Drug Abuse

OPPOSING VIEWPOINTS®

OTHER BOOKS OF RELATED INTEREST

OPPOSING VIEWPOINTS SERIES

Alcohol
Chemical Dependency
Tobacco and Smoking
Sports and Athletes
Teens at Risk
The War on Drugs

CURRENT CONTROVERSIES SERIES

Alcoholism
Drug Trafficking
Illegal Drugs
Teen Addiction

AT ISSUE SERIES

Legalizing Drugs
Marijuana

Drug Abuse

OPPOSING VIEWPOINTS®

James D. Torr, *Book Editor*
Scott Barbour, *Assistant Editor*
Jennifer A. Hurley, *Assistant Editor*

David L. Bender, *Publisher*
Bruno Leone, *Executive Editor*
Bonnie Szumski, *Editorial Director*
David Haugen, *Managing Editor*

OPPOSING
VIEWPOINTS®
SERIES

Greenhaven Press, Inc., San Diego, California

Cover photo: Photodisc

Library of Congress Cataloging-in-Publication Data

Drug abuse : opposing viewpoints / James D. Torr, book editor,
    Scott Barbour, assistant editor, Jennifer A. Hurley, assistant editor.
        p.   cm.
    Includes bibliographical references and index.
    ISBN 0-7377-0051-3 (lib. : alk. paper). —
ISBN 0-7377-0050-5 (pbk. : alk. paper)
    1. Drug abuse—United States. 2. Teenagers—Drug use—United
States. 3. Drug abuse—United States—Prevention. I. Torr, James D.,
1974–   . II. Barbour, Scott, 1963–   . III. Hurley, Jennifer A.,
1973–   .
HV5825.D7735 1999
362.29'0973—dc21   98-32056
                                                               CIP

Greenhaven Press, Inc., P.O. Box 289009
San Diego, CA 92198-9009

> # "CONGRESS SHALL MAKE NO LAW... ABRIDGING THE FREEDOM OF SPEECH, OR OF THE PRESS."
>
> First Amendment to the U.S. Constitution

The basic foundation of our democracy is the First Amendment guarantee of freedom of expression. The Opposing Viewpoints Series is dedicated to the concept of this basic freedom and the idea that it is more important to practice it than to enshrine it.

CONTENTS

WHY CONSIDER OPPOSING VIEWPOINTS?

> "The only way in which a human being can make some approach to knowing the whole of a subject is by hearing what can be said about it by persons of every variety of opinion and studying all modes in which it can be looked at by every character of mind. No wise man ever acquired his wisdom in any mode but this."
>
> **John Stuart Mill**

In our media-intensive culture it is not difficult to find differing opinions. Thousands of newspapers and magazines and dozens of radio and television talk shows resound with differing points of view. The difficulty lies in deciding which opinion to agree with and which "experts" seem the most credible. The more inundated we become with differing opinions and claims, the more essential it is to hone critical reading and thinking skills to evaluate these ideas. Opposing Viewpoints books address this problem directly by presenting stimulating debates that can be used to enhance and teach these skills. The varied opinions contained in each book examine many different aspects of a single issue. While examining these conveniently edited opposing views, readers can develop critical thinking skills such as the ability to compare and contrast authors' credibility, facts, argumentation styles, use of persuasive techniques, and other stylistic tools. In short, the Opposing Viewpoints Series is an ideal way to attain the higher-level thinking and reading skills so essential in a culture of diverse and contradictory opinions.

In addition to providing a tool for critical thinking, Opposing Viewpoints books challenge readers to question their own strongly held opinions and assumptions. Most people form their opinions on the basis of upbringing, peer pressure, and personal, cultural, or professional bias. By reading carefully balanced opposing views, readers must directly confront new ideas as well as the opinions of those with whom they disagree. This is not to simplistically argue that everyone who reads opposing views will—or should—change his or her opinion. Instead, the series enhances readers' understanding of their own views by encouraging confrontation with opposing ideas. Careful examination of others' views can lead to the readers' understanding of the logical inconsistencies in their own opinions, perspective on why they hold an opinion, and the consideration of the possibility that their opinion requires further evaluation.

EVALUATING OTHER OPINIONS

To ensure that this type of examination occurs, Opposing Viewpoints books present all types of opinions. Prominent spokespeople on different sides of each issue as well as well-known professionals from many disciplines challenge the reader. An additional goal of the series is to provide a forum for other, less known, or even unpopular viewpoints. The opinion of an ordinary person who has had to make the decision to cut off life support from a terminally ill relative, for example, may be just as valuable and provide just as much insight as a medical ethicist's professional opinion. The editors have two additional purposes in including these less known views. One, the editors encourage readers to respect others' opinions—even when not enhanced by professional credibility. It is only by reading or listening to and objectively evaluating others' ideas that one can determine whether they are worthy of consideration. Two, the inclusion of such viewpoints encourages the important critical thinking skill of objectively evaluating an author's credentials and bias. This evaluation will illuminate an author's reasons for taking a particular stance on an issue and will aid in readers' evaluation of the author's ideas.

As series editors of the Opposing Viewpoints Series, it is our hope that these books will give readers a deeper understanding of the issues debated and an appreciation of the complexity of even seemingly simple issues when good and honest people disagree. This awareness is particularly important in a democratic society such as ours in which people enter into public debate to determine the common good. Those with whom one disagrees should not be regarded as enemies but rather as people whose views deserve careful examination and may shed light on one's own.

Thomas Jefferson once said that "difference of opinion leads to inquiry, and inquiry to truth." Jefferson, a broadly educated man, argued that "if a nation expects to be ignorant and free . . . it expects what never was and never will be." As individuals and as a nation, it is imperative that we consider the opinions of others and examine them with skill and discernment. The Opposing Viewpoints Series is intended to help readers achieve this goal.

David L. Bender & Bruno Leone,
Series Editors

Greenhaven Press anthologies primarily consist of previously published material taken from a variety of sources, including periodicals, books, scholarly journals, newspapers, government documents, and position papers from private and public organizations. These original sources are often edited for length and to ensure their accessibility for a young adult audience. The anthology editors also change the original titles of these works in order to clearly present the main thesis of each viewpoint and to explicitly indicate the opinion presented in the viewpoint. These alterations are made in consideration of both the reading and comprehension levels of a young adult audience. Every effort is made to ensure that Greenhaven Press accurately reflects the original intent of the authors included in this anthology.

INTRODUCTION

"Although addiction is the result of voluntary drug use,
  addiction is no longer voluntary behavior, it's uncontrollable
  behavior."
  —Alan Leshner, director of the National Institute on Drug Abuse

"Drug addicts and alcoholics respond to rewards and
  consequences."
  —Sally Satel, psychiatrist at the Yale University School of Medicine

Drug abuse affects drug users, their families, and society as a whole. The National Institute on Drug Abuse (NIDA) estimates that drug abuse costs the United States as much as $246 billion each year. In calculating this figure, the institute attempts to account for the health care expenditures incurred by drug addicts, drug-related deaths, motor vehicle crashes, impaired workplace productivity, and crime. The NIDA notes that much of the cost of drug abuse falls on the families of drug abusers and victims of drug-related crime. Still, the institute's final tally does not reflect the suffering that drug abuse can cause.

Understandably, Americans consider drug abuse to be one of the most serious problems facing the country. A study by the Harvard University School of Public Health reports that half of the population believes the drug problem represents "a fundamental breakdown in the country's morals." The study reports that although a majority of Americans "see the War on Drugs as having failed thus far," two out of three say they would be willing to pay higher taxes to combat drug abuse.

According to the Harvard study, the most popular option for dealing with drug abuse is more severe penalties for the possession and sale of drugs. However, many people oppose simply punishing drug offenders. In *Drug War Politics: The Price of Denial*, Eva Bertram cites studies indicating that time in prison does little to deter drug use and that "what is worse, the prison environment may actually encourage drug use. Drugs are readily available in prison, and many people who enter prison as nondrug users end up using drugs by the time they leave."

The most popular alternative to punitive measures is treatment for drug offenders, either coupled with or as an alternative to incarceration. This is the idea behind drug courts, in which nonviolent drug offenders are sentenced to supervised treatment rather than prison. But while many people believe treatment is the best way to deal with drug abusers, others question the effectiveness of drug treatment programs. Moreover, people may not feel that drug rehabilitation is adequate punishment for drug-related crimes.

This ambiguity over how best to deal with drug abuse stems in part from the complexities of drug addiction. The threat of imprisonment can discourage people from using illegal drugs in the same way it discourages people from committing other crimes. Similarly, the law demands that crimes, drug-related or not, be punished. On the other hand, drug addicts often make irrational decisions; many people believe they are not in control of their own actions and are undeterred by fear of punishment. These two views of drug abuse lead to two different conclusions regarding drug policy. If drug abuse is a voluntary act, justice demands that it be punished; if it is an uncontrollable condition, compassion requires that it be cured.

"Let's separate initial drug use from addiction," says Alan Leshner, director of the National Institute on Drug Abuse. "Although addiction is the result of voluntary drug use," he says, "addiction is no longer voluntary behavior, it's uncontrollable behavior." Drug addiction, according to Leshner, "is the result of drugs changing your brain in fundamental ways." Drugs produce their euphoric effects by stimulating the release of dopamine in the brain. But with repeated drug use, dopamine levels fall. The result, says Leshner, is that "eventually, the drugs decrease the person's ability to experience pleasure without the drug." Addiction, he says, "is literally a disease of the brain."

He believes this view of addiction has profound implications for drug policy. Leshner hopes that if people understand drug abuse and addiction as a medical condition rather than a criminal problem, support for treatment programs will increase. "Treatment of addiction is an important area for current and future research," Leshner says. His view of drug addiction also suggests the potential tõ treat addicts with other drugs that would help return dopamine levels and other chemical pathways in the brain to normal.

However, the NIDA position on drug abuse has its critics. William R. Miller and Sandra R. Brown, writing in *American Psychologist*, state that "there is every reason to view substance abuse primarily as a *behavior* that responds to the same psychological principles that govern behavior problems more generally," and they cite studies showing that the success of treatment programs is influenced by the addict's employment status and family environment. Moreover, "drug addicts and alcoholics respond to rewards and consequences, not just to physiology," says psychiatrist Sally Satel. She cites a University of St. Louis study which found that 85 percent of heroin addicts returning from Vietnam were able to quit the drug once they came home, indicating that cultural factors, the higher price of the drug, and fear of arrest helped them end their addiction.

Satel believes that viewing drug addiction as an uncontrollable behavior is not only incorrect, but potentially damaging as well: "The message that addiction is chronic and relapse inevitable is demoralizing to patients and gives the treatment system an excuse if it doesn't serve them well." She advocates treatment but prefers calling addiction a behavioral condition. "The person, not his autonomous brain, is the instigator of his relapse and the agent of his recovery," she maintains. In this view, treatment is important but punitive measures may also help deter drug abuse.

The relative emphasis that should be placed on treatment of drug addicts versus punishment of drug offenders is one of the issues debated in *Drug Abuse: Opposing Viewpoints*. This anthology explores the extent of the drug problem and how it can be dealt with in the following chapters: How Serious a Problem Is Drug Abuse? What Programs Are Effective in Reducing Drug Abuse? Is U.S. Drug Policy Effective in Dealing with Drug Abuse? Should Illegal Drugs Be Legalized? Drug abuse exacts a terrible price on individuals, families, communities, and the nation. By presenting a wide variety of opinions on the topic, this book aims to give the reader an understanding of the issues surrounding drug abuse and why efforts to deal with the problem are often so controversial.

CHAPTER 1

HOW SERIOUS A PROBLEM IS DRUG ABUSE?

CHAPTER PREFACE

Drug use is part of American culture. Hundreds of drug products are available for personal use at any local pharmacy. Millions of people use a stimulant every morning when they drink a cup of coffee. Many Americans consume alcoholic beverages, not only at parties and bars but also at formal celebrations such as weddings, and alcohol is often used symbolically by Christians and Jews.

Unfortunately, drug abuse is also part of American culture. Differentiating between drug use and drug abuse is not always easy, and a variety of criteria are often used to determine if a person is using or abusing drugs.

For many people, medical need is the key determinant in deciding whether a drug is being abused. In this view, the only legitimate use of drugs is for improving one's health or well-being; the use of a drug for any nonmedical reason is a form of drug abuse. The idea that medical use is not drug abuse figures prominently in the debate over legalizing marijuana for medical purposes in Arizona and California.

Others define drug abuse as the use of any illegal drug. Supporters of this view say that illicit drugs are prohibited because they are harmful; any use of them is dangerous. Moreover, whether or not they have the potential for other uses, illegal drugs are often taken purely for their mind-altering effects, such as relaxation or euphoria. Many people believe the recreational use of drugs is irresponsible or immoral and constitutes a form of drug abuse.

Still others believe drug use becomes drug abuse only when it results in social, economic, psychological, or legal problems for the user. This is a view commonly taken toward alcohol: Drinking in moderation may be considered acceptable, but it is deemed abuse if the drinking becomes excessive, if the user becomes dependent on alcohol, or if drinking interferes with the user's health, relationships with others, or obligations to work or school. Supporters of this definition of drug abuse may also condone recreational drug use and the use of illicit drugs.

The authors of the viewpoints in this chapter debate the extent to which drugs are used and abused by teens and adults, and also discuss the relative dangers of some of the popular drugs of abuse.

> "It's clear that the problem of substance abuse is immense."

DRUG ABUSE IS A SERIOUS PROBLEM

Michelle Johnson

Michelle Johnson, a former editorial manager of Boston.com, the *Boston Globe*'s on-line news site, created and heads her own Internet consulting firm. In the following viewpoint, Johnson argues that the problem of substance abuse is widespread in American society, resulting in huge economic and human costs. According to Johnson, drug abuse not only harms individuals who use drugs, but also contributes to social problems such as domestic violence, child abuse, and crime.

As you read, consider the following questions:

1. According to Johnson, how can a mother's drug abuse during pregnancy affect her child?
2. How do drugs and alcohol adversely affect the school environment, as explained by the author?
3. What percentage of illicit drug users are employed, as reported by Johnson?

Reprinted, with permission, from "Substance Abuse Overview," by Michelle Johnson, May 1998, taken from Join Together Online, www.jointogether.org.

S ome 18 million Americans abuse or are addicted to alcohol. Tobacco causes 400,000 deaths each year, killing more people than AIDS, alcohol, drug abuse, car crashes, suicides, and fires combined. And nearly half of all Americans say they know someone with a drug problem.

The toll of substance abuse can be measured in lost lives and dollars spent dealing with its effects. Each year there are more deaths and disabilities from substance abuse than from any other preventable cause. Of 2 million US deaths each year, one in four is attributable to alcohol, illicit drug, or tobacco use.

The cost of dealing with illicit drugs alone approaches $67 billion annually. Every man, woman and child in America pays nearly $1,000 a year to cover the costs of unnecessary health care, additional law enforcement, auto accidents, crime and lost productivity resulting from substance abuse.

The problematic use of alcohol, illicit drugs and tobacco places an enormous burden on society, harming health, family life, the economy and public safety. No segment of society is immune to its effects. . . .

AT HOME

Substance abuse can tear families apart, cause pain and injury, and lead to domestic violence, failed marriages, and child abuse and neglect. Studies show that one out of four Americans experience family problems related to alcohol abuse, and that it plays a part in one out of three failed marriages.

The link between substance abuse and domestic violence is well documented. According to a report in the May 1997 *Journal of the American Medical Association*, 92 percent of assailants in domestic violence cases used alcohol and/or drugs.

Reports of child neglect and abuse have increased rapidly in recent years, doubling between 1986 and 1993. Many of these incidents can be linked to illicit drug use and alcohol abuse. Children from many affected families end up in foster care. Some 500,000 children were in foster care in 1996. Drug abuse by a parent is a factor in more than three-quarters of foster care cases. Damage to children in families affected by substance abuse can begin early:

- Drug abusing mothers can give birth to drug-addicted babies;
- Women who contract HIV through intravenous drug use can pass the virus along to their children;
- Mothers who drink during pregnancy can have babies affected by fetal alcohol syndrome;

- Women who smoke can have children affected by low birth weight, and children whose parents smoke can suffer from a host of respiratory problems.

Untreated substance abuse can create a vicious cycle in families. Children's experience at home is the largest single factor in whether or not they will have a drug or alcohol problem early in life. The stress and pain from living in an alcohol- or drug-affected family can lead to the use of substances by other family members. In addition to all these ills, families suffer if money goes to support drug, alcohol, and tobacco habits in lieu of basic necessities.

AT SCHOOL: OUR YOUNG PEOPLE

Substance abuse is negatively affecting the quality of education in our nation's schools, from the elementary level, to college campuses. Students who drink, and use and sell drugs create an atmosphere that's dangerous and unsafe for other students and school staff. They're at risk of dropping out, and often lack motivation and self-discipline. And, they can be disruptive and violent when they're under the influence. Use of alcohol, illicit drugs, and tobacco is up among young people, and their concern about it is down.

Beginning in the early '90s, illicit drug use among junior- and high-school-aged students rose dramatically, more than doubling among 8th graders, according to the annual Monitoring the Future (MTF) survey. Use of marijuana, LSD, cocaine, and heroin has risen among 8th, 10th, and 12th graders since 1990. Meanwhile, studies show that attitudes about the perceived risks of illicit drug use among youth have declined steadily since 1991.

The good news: at least one new study shows the trend may be reversing. The National Household Survey on Drug Abuse released in August 1997 reports a slight drop in illicit drug use among 12–17 year olds. Although in recent years drug use among youth has been rising, it's not as high as it was in the late '70s, the peak of an epidemic. But if the trend of drug use among youth continues to rise, it could reach 1979 levels by 2001....

IN OUR COMMUNITIES

Substance abuse doesn't just hurt the abuser. Its effects echo throughout our communities, resulting in crime, unemployment, unsafe streets, and lost neighborhoods. The drug culture creates an atmosphere that spawns vandalism, homicides, theft and robbery. Drunk drivers maim and kill. And the costs are measured in thousands of lives lost and billions of dollars spent to deal with the ravages of this epidemic.

A few facts:

- Seventeen percent of 712,000 prison inmates interviewed in a 1991 study said that they were trying to get money for drugs when they committed the crime.
- Illicit drugs burden our society with approximately $67 billion in social, health, and criminal costs each year.
- Every year, at least 6,000 young people die in an event linked to alcohol. Eight die each day in alcohol-related crashes.
- The death toll from drug-related deaths in the '90s: 100,000.

THE CRIMINAL JUSTICE SYSTEM

Illicit drugs and alcohol are partners in crime. The link is visible every day in the nation's courtrooms, jails, and prisons. Of the $38 billion spent on prisons in 1996, more than $30 billion paid for the incarceration of individuals who had a history of drug and alcohol abuse, were convicted of drug and alcohol violations, were high on drugs and alcohol at the time of their crime, or committed their crime to get money to buy drugs, notes a recently released study by the National Center on Addiction and Substance Abuse (CASA).

Dick Wright. Reprinted by permission of United Feature Syndicate, Inc.

Most offenders who need addiction treatment don't receive it and are released into the community to commit additional crimes. According to CASA, state officials estimate that 70 to 85 percent of inmates need some level of substance abuse treatment. But in 1996, only 13 percent of state inmates received such treatment.

The Federal Bureau of Prisons estimates that 31 percent of their inmates are hooked on drugs, but only 10 percent were in treatment in 1996. Incarceration's not the only item on the bill for dealing with the criminal impact of substance abuse. Add to it the costs of arresting and prosecuting substance abusers. In 1995 it cost more than $5.2 billion to arrest and prosecute 1,436,000 DUI [driving under the influence] cases, according to CASA. . . .

IN THE WORKPLACE

A significant amount of substance abuse takes place among the American workforce, and some of this use occurs at work. Most illicit drug users are employed. In fact, 74 percent work, according to the 1996 National Household Survey on Drug Abuse. That survey also reports that three in four people who acknowledged using drugs in 1996 were employed, including 6.2 million full-time workers, and 1.9 million part-time workers.

One out of three Americans in the workforce smokes; eight percent drink alcohol daily; and 15 percent say they've used illicit drugs in the past year. The result: loss of productivity, higher absenteeism, increased health insurance costs, and risk of serious injury and death.

Among employed drug users, absenteeism is 66 percent higher, health benefit utilization is 84 percent greater in dollar terms, disciplinary actions are 90 percent higher, and there is significantly higher employee turnover. (Office of National Drug Control Policy, The National Drug Control Strategy, 1997)

AN IMMENSE PROBLEM

Substance abuse is a national problem, but defeating it requires the involvement of every concerned citizen on the local level. Individuals and organizations across the nation are successfully joining together in the fight against substance abuse. Parents and police, teachers and tavern owners, ministers and magistrates are developing action plans to turn their communities around.

It's clear that the problem of substance abuse is immense. And it's just as clear that any plan to fix it will need to cover a lot of bases. Every community must develop a comprehensive strategy for reducing alcohol, illicit drug and tobacco use, coordinated across institutions and among individual citizens.

"For every person who has died or
ended up in a gutter, millions have
dabbled in drugs and still led
productive . . . lives."

THE PROBLEM OF DRUG ABUSE IS EXAGGERATED

Seth Stevenson

In the following viewpoint, Seth Stevenson argues that government and media messages overstate the risks associated with using illegal drugs. Although Stevenson concedes that drugs can
ruin people's lives, he insists that most people are able to take
moderate amounts of drugs without suffering adverse consequences. Stevenson contends that media campaigns exaggerating
the harmfulness of drugs will backfire by causing young people
to mistrust adults and turn to their peers for advice. Stevenson is
a contributor to *Slate*, an on-line magazine published by Microsoft Corporation.

As you read, consider the following questions:

1. What does Stevenson consider the most shameful aspect of
   the media campaign by the Partnership for a Drug-Free
   America (PDFA)?
2. On what drugs should the PDFA focus its attention, in the
   author's opinion?
3. What facts regarding heroin and cocaine users do the
   antidrug ads ignore, according to Stevenson?

Reprinted from Seth Stevenson, "High and Mighty: The Lies of the Anti-Drug Propaganda
Machine," *Slate*, www.slate.com, July 23, 1998, with permission. Copyright ©1998
Microsoft Corporation.

There's a new It Girl on television these days—a pale, sexy, raccoon-eyed waif who looks like an advertisement for shooting heroin. The twist: The commercial is an ad for *not* shooting heroin. The waif smashes china and plumbing fixtures in the commercial, screaming angrily about how heroin will ruin your life.

The waif spot is one of a series of new anti-drug commercials that the government will pay $1 billion to air through 2002. The ads are produced by the Partnership for a Drug-Free America (PDFA)—the best funded and best connected propaganda machine in America today. It's backed by the president, the speaker of the House, both parties in Congress, the biggest of big corporations and foundations, the advertising industry, and the major media.

A BALDFACED LIE

The slickness and pervasiveness of the campaign conceals one flaw: The message—that all drug use leads to disaster—is a baldfaced lie.

Founded in 1986 by a group of advertising execs, the PDFA's stated goal is to produce and place ads that persuade kids not to try drugs, to "denormalize" adult drug use, and to make drug use "less acceptable." Its latest TV ads—created pro bono by leading ad agencies—will saturate prime time thanks to a budget in excess of what Nike or Sprint spent on TV advertising in 1997. (The PDFA once relied on donated airtime, but in these flush days network time is at a premium, hence the requisition of taxpayers' funds.) The budget dwarfs even the public service ad campaign run during World War II in support of the war effort.

The ads focus solely on kids. In addition to the waif ad is one that depicts a little girl answering questions. Lesson: Her mother has told her not to talk to strangers but hasn't told her drugs are bad. In another ad, a father and son sit at the breakfast table in silence. Lesson: This time could have been spent talking about how drugs are bad.

Some have attacked the efficacy of these ads. Indeed, no study conclusively demonstrates a link between them and reduced drug use. Few have slammed the hypocrisy of the politicians and the ad agency staffers behind this campaign, who can't all be drug virgins. But the greater scandal is the free pass that reporters, most of whom have imbibed, have granted the PDFA's propaganda blitz. (The lone exception is the *New York Times*' Frank Rich.)

Let's be clear: Drugs can be awful. They can destroy lives. But for every person who has died or ended up in a gutter, millions have dabbled in drugs and still led productive, sane, successful lives. This is indisputable. In fact, some long-term drug use can be harmless—and, yes, even kind of fun. But the PDFA model offers only the salvation of abstinence or the perdition of addiction. The PDFA's Web site suggests you tell your kids marijuana is "a bad drug that can hurt your body."

While it's true that marijuana smoke (like tobacco smoke) contains carcinogens and the medical data suggest it compromises the immune system and can also lead to short-term memory loss, honesty demands that the silent dad in the PDFA ad admit to his son that he smoked a good deal of pot when he was young, still occasionally lights up at parties, and has turned out just fine.

THE REAL LESSON

Republicans think kids are encouraged to use marijuana when they hear that the president's press secretary—not to mention the president—tried it when he was young. . . .

The real lesson of these confessions is not that drug use is morally acceptable. It's that, contrary to anti-drug propaganda, you can experiment with illicit drugs and still go on to live a successful and productive life.

Stephen Chapman, *Conservative Chronicle*, September 4, 1996.

Instead, the PDFA insists on using your tax dollars to lie to your kids. Should teens hate and fear a friendly, well-adjusted, responsible classmate who occasionally rolls a spliff? Should the culture denormalize someone who does good work in a steady job, hurts no one, and once in a blue moon sniffs some blow at a club? Are you on a hell-bound train if you take mushrooms? Is all drug use drug abuse? The PDFA tells your kids "yes" when the correct answer is "no."

Perhaps the most shameful thing about the PDFA propaganda campaign is that its leaders know better, having used drugs themselves. Bill "Didn't Inhale" Clinton, Newt Gingrich, and Al Gore have all admitted to having tried drugs in their early days. How can they tell kids pot is an evil gateway drug when they're stellar proof that it isn't? . . .

IGNORING THE SUBTLETIES

We don't trust Madison Avenue to tell us the truth about fabric softener, so why are we letting it brainwash our children about drugs? Indeed, if the PDFA had a shred of integrity, its ads would be battling alcohol and tobacco, America's two most injurious drugs and the two most popular among teens. (The PDFA no longer takes money from Philip Morris, RJR Reynolds, and Anheuser-Busch or other booze and smokes companies, but even so, the alcohol connection remains: Margeotes/Fertitta and Partners, which created the waif spot, also designs Stolichnaya vodka ads.)

In a rational world, the Republicans who decry the antitobacco campaign as another appendage of the nanny state would see through the PDFA campaign and reiterate their belief that Americans can be trusted to make informed choices. For instance, contrary to what the raccoon-eyed waif suggests, many heroin users are able to use their drugs and conduct functional lives. What makes heroin users' life so crazy is that their dependence on an illegal drug forces them to enter a criminal underworld. The PDFA ignores these subtleties. Likewise with cocaine: Most of the 22 million Americans who've tried it have had no trouble walking away from it. And pot? No one has *ever* overdosed.

By confusing propaganda with education, the PDFA stands to reap the whirlwind. We don't lie to kids about alcohol. Everyone knows from an early age what it can do—and that most people can handle liquor, but some people can't. Eventually kids see through the drug hysteria, usually by the time they turn 12 or 13 and start observing drug users for themselves. When they discover they've been lied to, they stop trusting the liar—their parents or teachers or TV commercials—and start trusting their peers. Whatever real opportunity we have to reach them vanishes. Simply letting kids know what the real risks are, without hyperbole, should be enough. Madison Avenue propaganda is counterproductive.

"Never before have American adolescents been asked to grow up amid such a combustible and dangerous mix of substance abuse conditions."

TEEN DRUG USE IS INCREASING

The National Center on Addiction and Substance Abuse (CASA)

The National Center on Addiction and Substance Abuse (CASA), located at Columbia University in Missouri, is a think tank devoted to combating drug abuse in American society. In the following viewpoint, excerpted from a report by the CASA Commission on Substance Abuse Among America's Adolescents, CASA states that the rate of drug use by teenagers has been increasing in recent years and that a growing number of teens are starting to use drugs before they reach adolescence. According to CASA, this rise in adolescent drug use has been caused in part by cultural messages that glamorize substance abuse.

As you read, consider the following questions:

1. What percentage of teens between fifteen and seventeen report that drugs are present at their school, according to CASA?
2. What evidence does CASA cite to support its contention that cigarettes, alcohol, and marijuana are gateway drugs?
3. What percentage of teens between twelve and seventeen have a friend who uses drugs, as reported by CASA?

Reprinted, with permission, from the 1997 National Survey of American Attitudes on Substance Abuse III: Teens and Their Parents, Teachers, and Principals, published by The National Center on Addiction and Substance Abuse (CASA), at www.casacolumbia.org/pubs/aug97/contents.htm.

A combination of factors makes substance abuse a more serious problem to American adolescents than ever before in our history. Never have so many substances of potential abuse been so widely available to young teens. Not surprisingly with such ready availability, from 1992 to 1996, teen substance use involving nicotine, marijuana, amphetamines, other illicit drugs like cocaine, heroin and acid and inhalants has been rising. Binge drinking has also begun to increase, particularly among younger teens. Marijuana use among teens doubled between 1993 and 1996, and the pot they're smoking is far more potent than that of the 1960s.

If drug use among teenagers continues at current rates or even if such use is slightly reduced, America will enter the new Millennium with more teenagers using drugs, since the number of adolescents is rising and continues to rise through the early years of the next century. The number of teens age 12 to 17 will increase from 20.1 million to 23.6 million between 1990 and the year 2000, rising to 25 million by 2010.

DRUGS ARE READILY AVAILABLE

Teens report that they have little or no trouble obtaining beer and other alcohol. Sting operations using 12-year-olds consistently reveal how easily they can buy cigarettes. Many teens can get marijuana within a day; some say they can get it within a couple of hours. More than 70 percent of 15- to 17-year-olds report that drugs are used, sold and kept at their schools. The same proportion of parents of teenagers agree. With adults taking billions of mood altering pills each year, for most teens drugs are as close as their parents' medicine cabinet. Thanks to hundreds of products, from Reddi Wip and shaving cream to motor oil additives and spray cleaners, young adolescents can find an inhalant high in the kitchen cupboard, under the kitchen sink and on the garage shelf.

However measured—by average age, median age, proportion of 12-year-olds (and younger) using substances from beer and cigarettes to marijuana, pills and even heroin—the age of initiation of substance use has never been lower. Music, movies, television and fashion—where teens find out what's cool and chic to mimic—glamorize smoking, drinking and even some drug use, particularly marijuana smoking and, in many fashion ads, heroin. Too many baby boomer parents, survivors of pot smoking in their twenties and college years, send their kids mixed messages about substance abuse. These messages not only confuse teens; worse still, they sometimes signal that inhalant highs, binge drinking, smoking pot and puffing cigarettes are acceptable rites of passage for American adolescents. Unfortunately, many teens fail to make safe passage through such rites.

Over its history, America has been through cycles of drug and alcohol use and abuse. But never before have American adolescents been asked to grow up amid such a combustible and dangerous mix of substance abuse conditions—increased use and abuse by their peers, experimentation and abuse at younger ages, the widespread availability of all kinds of drugs to children and teens, the cultural glamorization of cigarettes, alcohol and drugs, drug-ridden public and private high schools. These conditions flourish in a time of serious concern about the quality of family life, deteriorating public education (particularly in urban centers) and weakening moral values.

ISOLATING THE EFFECTS OF GATEWAY DRUGS

The increased teen use of cigarettes, marijuana and alcohol is troubling in and of itself. Indeed, Dr. Alan Leshner, director of the National Institute on Drug Abuse, estimates that each year more than 100,000 individuals seek treatment for their marijuana dependence. Most of them are teens. But such use may also signal an increased likelihood of use of other drugs like heroin and cocaine. In October 1994, the National Center on Addiction and Substance Abuse (CASA) reported on its extensive statistical analysis demonstrating the greater likelihood that 12- to 17-year-olds who smoked, drank and used marijuana would use cocaine. That study did not isolate use of these gateway substances from other problem behavior such as violence, crime, truancy or sexual promiscuity. As a result, that study was not able to measure the relationship of smoking, drinking and marijuana use in and of themselves, to use of harder drugs.

For the first time, CASA has been able to isolate smoking, drinking or using marijuana from other problem syndromes. When smoking, drinking and using marijuana are isolated from other problem behaviors, the statistical relationships are powerful:

- Among 12- to 17-year-olds with no other problem behaviors, those who report drinking alcohol and smoking cigarettes at least once in the past month are 30 times likelier to smoke marijuana than those who report neither smoking nor drinking alcohol.
- Compared to teens who report using none of the three gateway drugs (cigarettes, alcohol and marijuana) in the past month, teens who have used all three are almost 17 times likelier to have used a harder drug like cocaine,

heroin or acid.

- Teenage boys who report using cigarettes, alcohol and marijuana at least once in the past month are 29 times likelier to have used a harder drug like cocaine, heroin or acid than boys who report using none of these gateway substances.
- Teenage girls who report using cigarettes, alcohol and marijuana at least once in the past month are 11 times likelier to have used a harder drug like cocaine, heroin or acid than girls who report using none of these gateway substances.

These relationships are only statistical. But they are far more compelling than the initial findings in the first Surgeon General's Report On Smoking and Health that those who smoked cigarettes were nine to ten times likelier to get lung cancer than those who didn't, and the early Framingham heart study findings that individuals with high cholesterol were two to four times likelier to have heart attacks.

Reprinted by permission of Ed Gamble.

Moreover, recent scientific studies here and in Europe have found that marijuana, nicotine and alcohol produce similar kinds of changes in brain chemistry as cocaine, heroin and amphetamines do. All these drugs affect dopamine levels through common pathways in the brain: one pathway is responsible for the high and another pathway for the anxiety brought on by withdrawal.

Friends Who Use Drugs

The increase in marijuana use over the past several years has been accompanied by a smaller but significant increase in adolescent use of drugs like heroin, cocaine and acid. Each year, CASA conducts a national survey of attitudes toward substance abuse. The 1997 survey also included middle and high school teachers as part of CASA's effort to assess the attitudes of those who influence our teens. One finding of the survey is [especially] pertinent: the percentage of 12- to 17-year-olds who have a friend or classmate who uses drugs like cocaine, heroin or acid rose by more than 40 percent between 1996 and 1997.

In 1996, 12- to 17-year-olds were asked if they had a friend or classmate who used drugs like cocaine, heroin or acid: 39 percent knew friends or classmates who used such drugs. In the 1997 survey, 56 percent knew a friend or classmate who uses cocaine, heroin or acid. Among 12-year-olds, the increase was even greater, more than doubling from 10.6 percent to 23.5 percent.

Our nation need not accept the widespread availability of nicotine, alcohol and drugs among teens and we recommend some actions to help curb that availability. Efforts to interdict drugs at our borders can be more effective. Mayor Rudolph Guiliani and local police, working with federal and state law enforcement agencies, have cut drug availability and crime in New York City; other cities can mount similar efforts. Reducing availability of cigarettes, alcohol and drugs is essential.

Helping Teens Say "No"

Nevertheless, we must recognize that in a free society, such substances are likely to be available to any teen who wants to get them. Let's face it: every American 12- to 17-year-old—and some children much younger—will be called upon to make a conscious choice whether to smoke, drink or use drugs before they graduate from high school. And American teens will face that choice in situations where the substances are immediately at hand and being used by their peers.

That's why it is critical to put a premium on helping teens develop the skill and will to say no and to not want to use drugs. That responsibility falls squarely on those who have the greatest influence on adolescents: parents, teachers, peers, clergy, doctors, and the trend-setting entertainment, fashion and advertising industries. . . .

How teens deal with substance use and abuse will be determined in the first instance in their homes, schools and communities, among their peers and in their extra-curricular and religious activities and leisure pursuits. The responsibility that parents, teachers and others who influence what teens do and how they act cannot be overstated. But there are important roles for government. At every level, government has a critical obligation to promote the public health, to deliver messages about substance abuse and addiction clearly and persuasively. The National Institutes of Health bear key responsibility to step up research in addiction and adolescence. Our Commission asks the nation and government leaders to commit themselves to developing techniques that will motivate teens to pursue healthy lifestyles and stay away from nicotine, alcohol and drugs that can harm and addict them. It's time for America to make a major research investment in its adolescents and the greatest threat they face.

| "The fact is that teenagers ... have not been a major part of the national drug problem for more than 15 years."

TEEN DRUG USE IS NOT INCREASING

Mike Males

In the following viewpoint, Mike Males challenges reports that drug use by American adolescents has increased. Males insists that, contrary to the claims of government officials and the media, drug use among teenagers is lower today than it was in the early 1970s; moreover, Males asserts, teens make up an extremely small proportion of those who die from drug abuse. Rather than exaggerating the problem of drug abuse among young people, according to Males, policy makers should focus on the more serious problem of adult drug abuse. Males is the author of *The Scapegoat Generation: America's War on Adolescents*.

As you read, consider the following questions:

1. What evidence does Males cite to support his view that the war on drugs is failing?
2. Why do officials avoid discussing the worsening problem of adult drug abuse, according to the author?
3. How does Males respond to Joseph Califano's assertion that teens who smoke marijuana are likely to try cocaine?

Reprinted from Mike Males, "High on Lies: The Phony 'Teen Drug Crisis' Hides the Deadly Truths of the 'War on Drugs,'" *Extra!* September/October 1995, by permission of *Extra!*

Former White House Office of Drug Control advisor Suzanne Miller, writing in Orange County's edition of the *Los Angeles Times* (5/3/95), emotionally recapped a "sun-kissed Southern California teenage couple" killed by crystal methedrine—another tale in the government and media roadshow of the "rising adolescent drug crisis."

Even in crowded, sun-kissed dope-land, Miller had to scour hard to find a teenage drug death. In Southern California's eight-county, 20-million-person sprawl, only 12 teens aged 13–19 died from drug overdoses in 1993. For those who believe surveys, youth drug-taking is far less common today than in the early '70s, when two-thirds of the Baby Boom kids were indulging bong, tab and pill.

But a true picture is hazardous to official health. The bitter results of one of America's worst social policy disasters, the decade-old "War on Drugs," are ones that officials are loath to discuss—and a submissive media is yet to report.

The fact is that teenagers, the eternal whipping-decoys trotted out by anti-drug forces, have not been a major part of the national drug problem for more than 15 years. In California and the U.S. as a whole, teens are the *least* likely of any age group except children to die from drug abuse.

But the never-modest drug war can't take credit for the teen drug death decline, all of which occurred prior to its launching. In fact, since the drug war was declared by President Ronald Reagan in 1983 and revved up with billions in congressional funding in 1986, the teen drug toll has risen by 25 percent (though the numbers remain tiny: around 100 deaths in 1983, 120 in 1993).

THE ADULT DRUG PROBLEM

But there is indeed a major, exploding drug problem in the U.S.—one inconvenient for anti-drug warriors. In the last dozen years, drug deaths have risen 80 percent among adults, primarily middle-aged men of all races, and today stand at record-high levels.

In 1983, the year the modern drug war began, 3,900 Americans died from drug overdoses (National Center for Health Statistics, *Vital Statistics of the U.S.*) and 500 in drug-related murders (FBI, *Uniform Crime Reports*). In 1993, after 10 million drug arrests and hundreds of billions spent on law enforcement, education, treatment, interdiction and increasingly harsh punishments, 7,200 Americans died from drug overdoses and 1,900 in drug-related murders—the highest rates in this century and probably all time.

Overdose deaths and drug murders are not the totality of drug abuse, but they're good indexes of where the most serious problems lie. The stark figures point to a tough, simple question the media should be asking: Given that the rationale for the drug war is to curb drug abuse and crime, how can officials claim success when drug abuse deaths have doubled and drug murders tripled?

Drug officials can be candid when asked. "Unless you're blind to this [rising death], you can't help but be concerned about it," U.S. Drug Enforcement Administration spokesperson Roger Guevara readily acknowledged when I asked why officials hype casual pot surveys but ignore real drug casualties. "It's almost like we're talking out of both sides of our mouths."

But the media don't ask. Government officials hired to produce ever-scarier "kids 'n' drugs" headlines have diverted media attention to trivial matters with ease, convincing journalists to fixate on self-reported, occasional use of mild drugs by students.

In election-year 1988, for example, when proving "success" was the goal, smiling bureaucrats handed out press releases featuring University of Michigan surveys of declining adolescent dope-taking. The Reagan administration didn't mention the rising drug-related death and violence tolls, clearly evident in government reports, and won scores of laudatory press accounts.

"The message is out, and America's young people have heard it," Reagan beamed (*L.A. Times*, 1/17/88). Health Secretary Otis Bowen gave full credit to the "just say no" campaign (*New York Times*, 1/14/88). Other media ran similar stories of "winning" the school drug battle (States News Service, 1/18/88; United Press International, 1/25/88; *MacNeil/Lehrer NewsHour*, 5/18/88).

EXPLOITING ADOLESCENTS

However deceptive, the successful late-'80s government P.R. [public relations] pales beside the crude falsehoods of the '90s. As political and media attention waned, anti-drug officials once again turned to exploiting adolescents to mask now-obvious calamities riddling national policy.

To any reporter who bothers to open a recent, easily available vital statistics report, the enormous and rising drug toll among middle-aged men stands out like the Grand Tetons on the Wyoming prairie. Teenagers are a barely discernable blip, accounting for fewer than 2 percent of all drug deaths.

Southern California's figures are representative. In 1993, 10 children and 12 teens died from drug abuse—compared to 1,096 adults aged 20 or over. Six in 10 drug deaths today involve men aged 30 to 50. And despite media and law enforcement furor over non-whites and "crack" cocaine, 55 percent of the men and 70 percent of the women claimed by drugs in California are non-Latino whites—and white deaths involve heroin, illicit medical drugs and cocaine.

The gap is even more striking when one considers the inequities of the criminal justice system: In California, a white, middle-aged adult is five times more likely to die from drug abuse than is a black teenager, but is only one-tenth as likely to be arrested for drugs.

Thus 98 percent of the nation's illicit drug death toll are adults (not teens), two-thirds are whites (not minorities), and more than half involve medical (not street) drugs. Does this reality in any way resemble the officially propagated image of the nation's "drug crisis" as faithfully reflected in the media?

Of course not, and for obvious reasons: Openly discussing the rising, record adult drug carnage would require serious scrutiny of the failure of anti-drug policies and other misplaced social priorities. In contrast, teens are a guaranteed-easy media snowjob requiring little more than theatricality.

BLAMING CULTURAL MESSAGES

As Health and Human Services Secretary Donna Shalala and Education Secretary Richard Riley proved yet again at the December 1994 annual press splash, the media will hype "teen drug crises" blamed on druggie T-shirts, Dr. Dre and Black Crowes' lyrics, "glorification of marijuana and other drug use by a number of rock, grunge and rap groups," and other silliness—while letting officials off the hook for the grim national drug toll.

U.S. News & World Report's account (12/26/94) was typical of the take-a-memo repetition of official lines: "The 'just say no' campaigns of the 1980s worked: Most teens concluded that drugs were for losers." But given today's "caps and shirts adorned with the marijuana leaf" which "are fashionable mainstays in schools across the land," and the truism that teenagers slavishly emulate rock stars (except all the musicians telling them not to use drugs), it "should come as no surprise" that "now the glamour is back," *U.S. News* declared.

Gannett News Service (12/13/94) blamed "ominous" and "dangerous" marijuana trends on "cultural messages." ABC News reporter Carole Simpson (12/12/94) united with authorities in "an urgent call" for teenagers to "stop using drugs."

"Nearly 50 percent of 12th graders linked to drug use," the *L.A. Times* announced (12/13/94)—referring mainly to the kind of casual experimentation that failed to wreck the careers of Bill Clinton, Al Gore, Newt Gingrich and Clarence Thomas, whose highs and non-inhalings went on back when many kids really did die from dope.

TEEN DRUG USE IN PERSPECTIVE

Today's teens are much less likely to die of a drug overdose than were their 1970s counterparts. . . . In California, 134 teenagers died from accidental overdoses in 1970; in 1994, only 14 did. . . .

Teen drug use is still much lower today than it was in the late 1970s and early 1980s. High school seniors in 1985 were three times more likely than their peers in 1996 to be cocaine users. Even with the post-1992 rise in marijuana use, pot smoking hasn't reached the levels of the late 1970s. In 1996, 22 percent of high school seniors said they had smoked marijuana or hashish in the month before the survey; in 1978, 37 percent said they had.

David Whitman, U.S. News & World Report, May 5, 1997.

The media have unquestioningly accepted the official line that the "casual marijuana use, single-time marijuana use" that Shalala lambasted is more crucial than thousands of adult corpses from medical drug, heroin and cocaine overdose. Reporters highlighted anti-drug crusader Joseph Califano's claim that student pot smokers are "85 times likelier to use cocaine" than abstainers (CNN, 12/12/94), but failed to report that the survey itself showed six out of seven high school seniors who smoked pot had never used cocaine, and 97 percent had not done so in more than a year.

When the U.S. Supreme Court ruled on June 26, 1995, that, in effect, simply being an adolescent is reason enough for school authorities to suspect a drug habit and demand urine samples, this brought another round of media regurgitation of claims that officials were "winning the war against drugs among young people" in the '80s, but that now a new "crisis" had erupted (L.A. Times, 6/27/95; New York Times, 6/27/95). Media reports didn't mention that the Oregon school district involved in the case spent $15,000 in four years drug-testing 500 students—and only 12 tested positive.

NO HONEST DISCUSSION

If media factually reported the deadly legacy of the War on Drugs—25,000 more Americans dead from drug-related violence and overdoses over a decade than pre-war drug death rates would have predicted—then teenagers and the adult public could reasonably discuss whether there is more to fear from anti-drug hysteria than there ever was from drug use itself. But no honest discussion is taking place, and too-tame media are to blame.

The issue is no longer one of the news media publicizing a few harmless fibs to bolster a well-meaning, bipartisan government morality crusade. Rather, it is whether there are any limits to how much and how long the media will consort with a corrupted drug policy founded in deadly distortions and carnival diversions.

Ironically, former Defense Secretary Robert McNamara's recent Vietnam memoir, In Retrospect, warned of the price of press complicity with popular wars. One journalist has already spotted the link.

"The better newspapers are portraying the drug quagmire the way they once portrayed the quagmire in Vietnam," former New York Times editor Max Frankel wrote in the Times' Sunday magazine (12/18/94): "The brass that's bragging about progress and calling for still more troops, weapons, prisoners and money"; the media "too generous with pictures of prosecutors and politicians" touting "meaningless" drug arrests and drug seizures "much like the Vietnam body count."

"Not until we in the media do a better job of reporting the horrendous costs of this unwinnable war will the public consider alternative policies," Frankel wrote. The major media must come to believe "that the country is ready to hear unvarnished truth, like Walter Cronkite's passionate declaration in 1968 that it was time to get out of Vietnam."

But today's "unvarnished truth" is that ill-motivated authorities are waging open war against youths and minorities and compliant media are leading the cheers. With Cronkite himself as a full-fledged spokesperson for the drug war, narrating emotional ads about "kids and crack," there is no light at the end of the tunnel.

| "One out of every ten 8th graders and one out of every five 10th graders are using marijuana at least once a month."

MARIJUANA USE BY ADOLESCENTS IS A SERIOUS PROBLEM

Center for Substance Abuse Prevention

The Center for Substance Abuse Prevention (CSAP) is an agency within the Substance Abuse and Mental Health Services Administration of the U.S. Department of Health and Human Services. It is charged with leading the national effort to prevent alcohol, tobacco, and illicit drug problems. In the following viewpoint, the CSAP reports that marijuana use is increasing among adolescents. Using marijuana seriously impedes teenagers' ability to develop into healthy, well-adjusted adults, states the CSAP. Therefore, the organization concludes, the trend of increased marijuana use poses a threat to the nation's teens as well as to the communities in which they live.

As you read, consider the following questions:

1. What three possible reasons does the CSAP offer for recent trends in marijuana use among teenagers?
2. What is the average age of first use of marijuana, as reported by the CSAP?
3. How does marijuana affect the human reproductive system, according to the CSAP?

Excerpted from "Marijuana Backgrounder: What You Should Know," a publication of the U.S. Dept. of Health and Human Services, Substance Abuse and Mental Health Services Administration, Center for Substance Abuse Prevention, 1998.

On the face of it, marijuana may seem like a harmless drug. However, it is a drug that can kill initiative and drive, adversely affect short-term memory, and harm relationships. Marijuana use makes it easier for a young person to become involved in a "drug culture." And combining marijuana with high rates of school failure, HIV/AIDS, and violence provides a dangerous mix for youth.

On average, one in four youths entering detention tests positive for marijuana. Youth-against-youth violence is escalating—with 24 percent of juvenile homicide victims (whose assailants were known) having been murdered by another juvenile. In this environment there is potential for enormous suffering and loss.

MARIJUANA USE IS NOT HARMLESS

Marijuana is often mixed with other drugs such as PCP, is used in combination with alcohol and crack cocaine, and is increasingly used by children and young adolescents. These facts remind us that marijuana use is not as harmless as some might think. For example, in Atlanta, there is a reported increase in marijuana use among crack cocaine users. Approximately one-half of the dual-drug users report smoking the two drugs simultaneously, while the other half prefer to smoke marijuana after smoking crack cocaine. And according to the latest Parents Resource Institution on Drug Education (PRIDE) survey, more than 75,000 children in 6th grade already have tried marijuana.

In addition to these concerns, the latest data show that young people do not perceive great harm in using drugs. According to data accumulated over the past 20 years, the likelihood of using a drug is affected by one's perceptions of harm associated with the drug. For example, between 1975 and 1978, as fewer high school seniors perceived great harm in using marijuana, there was a steady increase in the rate of use. This trend began to reverse in 1979, when greater percentages of seniors reported increased perception of harm in use, which translated to a steady decrease. According to recent research, the latest increase in marijuana use among youth was both preceded and accompanied by a decrease in perceived risk of use.

According to social scientists, there are several possible reasons for this recent trend. First, given the overall lower rates of use, fewer young people today have opportunities to observe firsthand the effects of heavy marijuana use among their peers. Second, media coverage of harmful effects of drugs and incidents resulting from drug use (particularly marijuana) has decreased substantially in recent years. And third, part of the problematic nature of marijuana is the false general perception that it is not "bad" for you and that it boosts creativity. These misperceptions are often reinforced in rock and rap music, with the recent resurgence of "pot" themes in songs containing lyrics promoting marijuana use. Such misperceptions can lead to a rapid deterioration of the hard-won gains we have made since the late 1970's. We must act now to ensure that this deterioration will not happen.

A DISTURBING TREND

Let's take a look at some of the data so that we fully understand how the use of marijuana and other drugs is creating a troubling and growing drug culture among America's youth.

In 1979, current (past month) use of illegal drugs among adolescents peaked at 18 percent. It went down by 1982, rose slightly until 1985, and then declined constantly to approximately 7 percent of all youth between the ages of 12 and 17 in 1991. Now a resurgence has occurred in illegal drug use among adolescents. According to the 1997 Monitoring the Future survey, current illicit drug use for 8th graders was about 5.7 percent in 1991 but jumped to 12.9 percent in 1997; for 10th graders, illicit drug use increased from 11.6 percent in 1991 to 23 percent in 1997; and among 12th graders, illicit drug use increased from 16.4 percent in 1991 to 26.2 percent in 1997.

The story is slightly different for marijuana. The number of new users has been increasing since 1988. By 1992, an estimated 1.6 million people joined the ranks of marijuana smokers. Current use among 12- to 17-year-old males is 7.6 percent and among 12- to 17-year-old females, 6.6 percent. More disturbing is that the average age of first use of marijuana is 13.9 years.

Marijuana use among young adolescents is especially disturbing. According to the literature, because adolescence is a period of important and necessary physical, psychological, and cognitive development, those who use drugs during this time are more likely to experience more severe problems related to their drug use.

Among 8th graders, increases in lifetime and annual use of marijuana first reported in 1992 continued through 1997. Between 1992 and 1997, lifetime use increased from 11.2 percent to 22.6 percent; annual use increased from 7.2 percent to 17.7 percent; and current use increased from 3.7 percent to 10.2 percent.

Among 10th graders, lifetime use of marijuana increased from 21.4 percent in 1992 to 42.3 percent in 1997. Annual use increased from 15.2 percent in 1992 to 34.8 percent in 1997, and current use increased from 8.1 percent in 1992 to 20.5 percent in 1997. One out of every ten 8th graders and one out of every five 10th graders are using marijuana at least once a month. And according to the latest survey, nearly one out of every four high school seniors uses marijuana.

IS EXPERIMENTATION NORMAL?

Some might say that this finding lends credence to the idea that it is either natural or normal that young people will experiment with drugs, especially with marijuana.

Many people forget that in the past, high rates of marijuana and other drug use contributed to many problems in society, including

- young people dropping out of school;
- adolescents failing to learn important interpersonal coping skills;
- problematic relationships between parents and their children;
- poor role modeling for younger siblings; and
- young people's decreasing ability to make appropriate decisions, solve problems, and learn new, developmentally appropriate skills.

MEMORY AND MOTIVATION

THC, the active ingredient in marijuana, has been shown to affect the learning process negatively. It disrupts the nerve cells in the part of the brain where memories are formed, making it hard for the user to recall what he or she just learned. A working short-term memory is required for learning and performing tasks that call for more than one or two steps. Memory is particularly important for our current technology-based economy, in which science and math skills are increasingly needed.

Some frequent, long-term marijuana users show signs of a lack of motivation (amotivational syndrome). Their problems include not caring about what happens in their lives, no desire to work regularly, fatigue, and lack of concern about how they look. As a result of these symptoms, some users tend to perform poorly in school or at work.

Clearly, marijuana is destructive to effective learning, school performance, and the self-image of the very young user.

Even though most marijuana smokers do not go on to use other illegal drugs, studies show that using marijuana puts children and teens in contact with people who are users and sellers of other drugs. In addition, they are faced with more peer pressure to use other substances.

Again, it is important to remember that marijuana often is used in a variety of ways with other substances, such as PCP, crack cocaine, and alcohol. . . .

LONG-TERM CONSEQUENCES

Studies indicate that marijuana use among youths ages 9 to 17 will be a greatly expanding population in the coming years.

Since younger adolescents are beginning to use marijuana, it is expected that there will be even more long-term consequences in the future.

Cancer. Studies show that someone who smokes five joints a week may be taking in as many cancer-causing chemicals as someone who smokes a full pack of cigarettes every day.

Respiratory System. Those who smoke marijuana regularly have many of the same respiratory problems that tobacco smokers have. They have symptoms of daily cough and phlegm (chronic bronchitis) and more frequent chest colds. Continuing marijuana smoking can lead to abnormal function of the lungs and airways.

Immune System. People with HIV/AIDS and others whose immune systems are impaired should avoid marijuana use because it is unclear how marijuana affects the immune system.

Reproductive system. Heavy marijuana use can affect hormones in both males and females, so it can affect bodily gender characteristics and reproductive function. Heavy doses of the drug may delay the onset of puberty in young men. Marijuana also can have adverse effects on sperm production.

Among women, regular marijuana use can disrupt the normal monthly menstrual cycle and inhibit the discharge of eggs from the ovaries.

Pregnancy. Smoking marijuana during pregnancy may cause damage to the unborn child. Preliminary findings from a 15-year study indicate that prenatal exposure to marijuana impairs decisionmaking, future planning, cognition (e.g., verbal reasoning and memory), and sustained attention among marijuana-exposed babies.

Dependence. A small percentage of users suffer withdrawal symptoms if they do not continue to use marijuana. More than 120,000 people entering drug treatment programs each year reported marijuana as their primary drug of abuse, showing they need help to stop using.

Perhaps the greatest concern associated with the increase we are seeing in marijuana use is not only the impact on individuals but the impact on relationships and on communities.

Adolescence is a time when young people learn the value of being a responsible citizen, a trusted friend, a respectful and useful son or daughter, and a loving girlfriend or boyfriend. They are separating from their childhood place in the family and taking on more independence that allows them to give back to the family in new and different ways. In the same fashion, they become part of the community through their participation in volunteer activities, school programs, sports, and other efforts.

8TH GRADE MARIJUANA USE

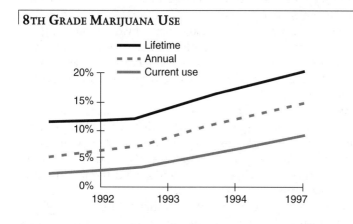

Source: National Institute on Drug Abuse, 1997.

What happens if young people skip these activities and start using marijuana and/or other drugs instead? What happens to those families? What happens to the relationship between teenagers and their friends? Between them and their girlfriends and boyfriends? What happens to the outlook for the community? Will it be a safe place for their younger brothers and sisters? What kind of foundation is being built? What support systems will be in place?

ADOLESCENCE IS NO TIME FOR DRUGS

As the Carnegie Council points out in its report *Great Transitions: Preparing Adolescents for a New Century*, adolescence is one of the most fascinating and complex transitions in the life span: a time of accelerated growth and change second only to infancy; a time of expanding horizons, self-discovery, and emerging independence; a time of metamorphosis from childhood to adulthood. There are numerous biological, physical, behavioral, and social transformations occurring. Young people are negotiating their way through a difficult transition made more difficult by the fact that they are often spending more of their time unsupervised by adults. They are also more vulnerable because of the increased risks they face for HIV/AIDS, homicide, suicide, teen pregnancy, and other problems. Many skills that will last a lifetime are being learned at this time to help youths navigate this transition and build the foundation upon which the rest of their lives will rest. It is no time for drugs.

The Carnegie Council report goes on to say that "nearly half of American adolescents are at high or moderate risk of seriously damaging their life chances."

The use of drugs can only make matters worse—not only for youth but for all of us. The youth of today are the community leaders and volunteers of tomorrow. An increase in marijuana or other drug use can create a negative impact on a community and its residents.

It is, therefore, in our best interest to help youth realize that marijuana use is illegal, harmful, and not acceptable. Pro-marijuana use messages are everywhere—on clothing, in music lyrics, and in movies. Young people need our help to counter these messages and images and to understand the facts regarding marijuana use.

Finally, helping young people to adopt healthful lifestyles is likely to result in significant savings in long-term health care costs and in increased workplace productivity. Young people who do not do drugs are more likely to stay in school and learn self-respect. They also are more likely to experience positive outcomes in life.

| "Claims of rapidly rising and near-epidemic rates of adolescent marijuana use hold little weight under close examination."

MARIJUANA USE BY ADOLESCENTS IS NOT A SERIOUS PROBLEM

Paul Armentano

Paul Armentano is director of publications for the National Organization for the Reform of Marijuana Laws (NORML), an organization that advocates legalizing marijuana. In the following viewpoint, Armentano responds to several claims made by policy makers and public health officials regarding marijuana use among teenagers. He maintains that although teen marijuana use may have increased slightly in recent years, the rise has been less dramatic than many experts claim. The rates of adolescent marijuana use are still below those of the late 1970s, the author points out. Armentano insists that NORML does not condone the use of marijuana by adolescents, but he believes that the problem should provoke only "mild concern."

As you read, consider the following questions:

1. How do the 1979 teen marijuana use rates compare with those of 1995, according to the author?
2. How does Armentano respond to the claim that teens are starting to use marijuana at a younger age?
3. In Armentano's opinion, what lesson should be taken from the alleged increase in teen marijuana use?

Reprinted from Paul Armentano, "Weeding Through the Hype: The Truth About Adolescent Marijuana Use," *Freedom @ NORML*, September 1996, by permission of the author. *Endnotes in the original have been omitted in this reprint.*

According to federal politicians, drug prohibitionists, and the majority of the national news media, adolescent marijuana use is dramatically on the increase and soaring toward epidemic proportions. This claim has been made so frequently that one may remain unaware there exists any serious debate on the issue. However, if one takes a closer look at the raw data, it becomes evident that there is little tangible evidence behind the current headlines. Consequently, it appears that this latest round of "reefer madness" is nothing more than a ploy to encourage legislators to stiffen penalties against adult users.

INACCURATE ASSERTIONS

Claim #1: Marijuana use among teens has doubled since 1992. There are several problems with this statement, the most obvious being that it is both misleading and inaccurate. The standard yardstick of adolescent marijuana use rates for more than 20 years has been the Monitoring the Future Report conducted at the University of Michigan Institute for Social Research. Each year, this study tracks the lifetime prevalence of marijuana use among high-school seniors. According to the study, in 1995, 42 percent of all high-school seniors had at one time in their lives experimented with marijuana. Admittedly, this figure is an increase over the 32.6 percent who reported having tried marijuana in 1992—the lowest year of reported lifetime use in the study's history—but it is hardly a doubling. In fact, current use rates are less than two percent higher than they were as recently as 1990 when prevalence stood at 40.7 percent.

Additional problems regarding this assertion come from the inherent limitations of self-reporting. Federal statistics regarding adolescent marijuana use are based upon teenagers' willingness to honestly self-report their use of an illicit substance. Therefore, one must take into account the fact that some teens may choose to either under-report or over-report their cannabis use depending on the social stigma or acceptance attached to marijuana at that time. For example, whereas an adolescent taking the survey in 1979 may have chosen to exaggerate his use of marijuana because of the societal notion that marijuana was "cool" and/or "hip," one taking the survey in 1985 may have under-reported his use because of the predominantly anti-marijuana social sentiment that existed at that time.

In addition, while most researchers admit that the results of self-reporting polls monitoring any activity should not be accepted at face value, polls that measure an individual's illicit drug consumption have been specifically criticized by the General Accounting Office (G.A.O.) for their "questionable" accuracy.

"Our national drug strategies are based on unsubstantiated and insufficient information," charged Rep. John Conyers (D-Mich.) after reviewing a 1993 G.A.O. report. "It is impossible to determine [from these surveys] whether . . . high school student drug use has been decreasing, increasing, or remaining stable."

USE RATES IN PERSPECTIVE

Claim #2: "Today, our children are smoking more dope . . . than at any time in recent memory," as stated by Bob Dole. Apparently, drug prohibitionists don't possess very long memories. Data from both the Monitoring the Future and the National Household Survey indicate that current rates of adolescent marijuana use, both regular and lifetime, are well below what they were just a few years ago. According to the Monitoring the Future Study, lifetime prevalence of marijuana use among high-school seniors peaked in 1979 at 60 percent, a figure that stands almost one-third higher than today's percentages. During this year, the percentage of youths aged 12–17 who reported regularly using marijuana (defined as once within the past month) to the National Household Survey on Drug Abuse also peaked, measuring 16.8 percent. Put in historical perspective, this figure is more than twice as high as today's reportedly "epidemic" 7.3 percent usage rate. Moreover, today's figure is only slightly higher than the percentage of adolescents who regularly consumed marijuana in 1988 (6.4 percent), a date prohibitionists laud as being at the height of the drug war and "just say no" campaign.

NO REASON FOR PANIC

When it comes to marijuana, we have good reason for concern when young kids start smoking, or when teenagers start to use it frequently. But reasons for concern are not reasons for panic or alarm, especially when kids are acting responsibly in other aspects of their lives.

Ethan A. Nadelmann, *Los Angeles Times*, January 3, 1997.

Claim #3: *Users are starting younger.* It is true that reports from the Monitoring the Future Study have indicated that marijuana use among 8th and 10th graders has been rising since 1992. However, this should come as little surprise because the study only began surveying 8th and 10th graders one year earlier. Not coincidentally, 1991 and 1992 were the lowest years ever recorded for adolescent marijuana use. Since then, use of marijuana has risen for adolescents of all ages. The truth is, we really don't know whether today's teens are using marijuana at a younger age because Monitoring the Future has no data from the 1970s or 1980s to compare it to. Moreover, to weigh today's figures against percentages of 8th and 10th graders taken in 1992—the year reported adolescent marijuana use rates stood at their lowest in history—serves little scientific purpose and is highly misleading.

MARIJUANA USE IS RELATIVELY HARMLESS

Claim #4: "Today's youthful marijuana users . . . are tomorrow's cocaine addicts," as stated by Sen. Orrin Hatch. According to the most recent literature from the National Institute on Drug Abuse (NIDA), the majority of marijuana users do not become dependent or move on to use other illegal drugs. This stands to reason when one realizes that an estimated 70 million Americans have experimented with marijuana at some point in their lives, the majority of whom never went on to use cocaine. Therefore, while it may be true that some cocaine users did first use marijuana as an adolescent, the far more important fact is that the overwhelming number of teen marijuana users never go on to use cocaine or any other illegal narcotic.

Claim #5: Adolescent marijuana use poses great harm to society. America survived the 1970s and America will survive the 1990s. While the National Organization for the Reform of Marijuana Laws (NORML) does not suggest that marijuana is totally harmless and certainly does not advocate that anyone—most especially adolescents—consume cannabis, the fact remains that moderate marijuana use is relatively harmless and poses far less cost to society than do the damaging effects of either cigarettes or alcohol. Today, as was the case in 1977 when President Jimmy Carter recommended federal marijuana decriminalization, far more harm is caused by the marijuana prohibition than by marijuana itself.

ONLY MILD CONCERN IS WARRANTED

Adolescent marijuana use should be a legitimate concern for all Americans. However, recently hyped claims about skyrocketing rates of adolescent marijuana use should be examined skeptically and must not be used to justify policies that would harshen penalties against adult users. If anything, recent data showing an increase in marijuana use among adolescents—if accurate—should serve as strong testimony to the failure and ineffectiveness of America's current drug education programs.

We may never truly know why adolescent marijuana use rates fluctuate over time or to what extent social stigmas and/or norms attached to cannabis may influence the accuracy of self-reporting. We do know that adolescence is a period filled with experimentation and that recreational marijuana use—for good or bad—is sometimes a part of this experience. Therefore, it is pertinent that young people, as well as all Americans, are informed of the scientific evidence about marijuana so that they can make knowledgeable decisions about both their own drug use and the future of American drug policy.

As this viewpoint demonstrates, the recent claims of rapidly rising and near-epidemic rates of adolescent marijuana use hold little weight under close examination. Furthermore, when put in historical perspective, today's figures warrant only mild concern. Most importantly, rates of adolescent marijuana use must not be used to intensify the war against adult marijuana consumers. We do not arrest responsible adult alcohol drinkers because we want adolescents to avoid alcohol, and neither can we as a nation justify arresting responsible adult marijuana smokers to protect our underage children from marijuana smoking. It is time to move beyond the current headlines and begin pursuing an enlightened policy that would stop treating adult marijuana consumers as criminals.

PERIODICAL BIBLIOGRAPHY

The following articles have been selected to supplement the diverse views presented in this chapter. Addresses are provided for periodicals not indexed in the *Readers' Guide to Periodical Literature*, the *Alternative Press Index*, the *Social Sciences Index*, or the *Index to Legal Periodicals and Books*.

Susan Crabtree	"The High Price of Drugs: Human Suffering and Death," *Insight*, April 21, 1997. Available from 3600 New York Ave. NE, Washington, DC 20001.
Glenn Ellen Duncan	"Shattered Dreams: The High Cost of America's Addiction," *Salt of the Earth*, January/February 1996. Available from 205 W. Monroe St., Chicago, IL 60606.
Tom Friend	"Teens and Drugs: Today's Youth Just Don't See the Dangers," *USA Today*, August 21, 1996.
Ted Gup	"Drugs and Crime," *Cosmopolitan*, July 1, 1996. Available from 224 W. 57th St., New York, NY 10019.
Joshua Hammer	"The War over Weed," *Newsweek*, March 16, 1998.
Alan I. Leshner	"Addiction Is a Brain Disease, and It Matters," *Science*, October 3, 1997.
Judy Monroe	"Marijuana—a Mind-Altering Drug," *Current Health*, March 1998.
Ethan A. Nadelmann	"Reefer Madness 1997: The New Bag of Scare Tactics," *Rolling Stone*, February 20, 1997.
Sarah Richardson	"Better Not Inhale," *Discover*, January 1998.
Sally Satel	"Don't Forget the Addict's Role in Addiction," *New York Times*, April 4, 1998.
Eric Schlosser	"More Reefer Madness," *Atlantic Monthly*, April 1997.
Cheryl Wetzstein	"Addiction Research Suggests Just Saying No Is Not Enough," *Insight*, September 22, 1997.
David Whitman	"The Youth 'Crisis,'" *U.S. News & World Report*, May 5, 1997.
Christopher S. Wren	"Phantom Numbers Haunt the War on Drugs," *New York Times*, April 20, 1997.

CHAPTER 2

WHAT PROGRAMS ARE EFFECTIVE IN REDUCING DRUG ABUSE?

CHAPTER PREFACE

In the late 1980s, a school district in Vernonia, Oregon, adopted a new program to crack down on teenage drug use. Maintaining that drug use was a serious problem among school athletes, the district made participation in athletics contingent upon an agreement to undergo urine tests. The program proceeded without complaint until 1991, when seventh grader James Acton refused to be tested as a condition of playing on the school football team. Acton's parents took the district to court, arguing that the rule infringed on their son's constitutional rights.

The Actons' case eventually reached the Supreme Court, where, in 1995, a majority upheld the school district's drug-testing program—a decision that outraged the American Civil Liberties Union (ACLU). According to the ACLU and others, testing students without any suspicion that they are using drugs constitutes an unreasonable search, which violates the Fourth Amendment. Furthermore, contend critics, drug-testing programs do not deter teenage drug abuse: The most likely effect of these programs, they claim, is a reduction in the number of drug-abusing student athletes, not a reduction in drug abuse as a whole. Columnist Stephen Chapman asserts that Vernonia's policy "may not have a great effect on drug abuse among adolescents, but it will teach them that they have no rights of privacy that the government is obliged to respect."

Defenders of Vernonia's program, in contrast, argue that drug tests are an effective method of preventing teenage drug use. Because student athletes act as role models for their peers, proponents say, mandating that athletes be drug-free prompts others to follow suit. As columnist Suzanne Fields states, the drug-testing policy "sends . . . strong incentives to students who need encouragement to abstain from drugs." In response to charges that Vernonia's program is unconstitutional, proponents maintain that since drug testing is only required by those who choose to participate in school sports, it does not violate any privacy rights.

Drug testing in schools and in the workplace is one approach to curbing the use of drugs. The following chapter presents opposing views on drug-testing programs and other controversial measures aimed at preventing and reducing drug abuse.

"More than 90% [of Drug *Abuse Resistance Education graduates*] *said they felt the program had helped them avoid drugs and alcohol.*"

DRUG EDUCATION DISCOURAGES ADOLESCENT DRUG ABUSE

Glenn Levant

In the following viewpoint, Glenn Levant argues that Drug Abuse Resistance Education (DARE), a worldwide drug education program implemented in U.S. public schools in 1983, discourages drug and alcohol use among adolescents. According to Levant, President and founding Director of DARE America, the program's curriculum provides students with the skills they need to resist peer pressure.

As you read, consider the following questions:

1. In Levant's view, what is the most important lesson DARE students learn?
2. According to the Gallup survey cited by Levant, what percentage of former DARE students have not tried drugs?
3. How much does it cost to send a child through the DARE program from kindergarten to twelfth grade, according to the author?

Reprinted from Glenn Levant, "Drug Prevention Works!" Texas D.A.R.E. Institute website: www.sherlock.tdi.swt.edu/DARE/Info, by permission of D.A.R.E. America.

Prevention programs have become the focus of more attention and support as the nation continues to grapple with . . . the rising human and financial cost of health care, violent crime, and drug abuse.

Prevention is a strategy that D.A.R.E. (Drug Abuse Resistance Education) has been using among young people since 1983.

As the nation's largest and most comprehensive drug-prevention and violence-avoidance education program, D.A.R.E. is recognized as an outstanding example of community based policing in which local schools, law enforcement, government, parents and communities work together to deal with this epidemic pro-actively. At a White House ceremony, first lady Hillary Rodham Clinton called D.A.R.E. a model that she wished could be replicated for other social issues.

What Is D.A.R.E.?

D.A.R.E. was founded in 1983 through a unique partnership between the Los Angeles Unified School District and the Los Angeles Police Department (LAPD). Starting with a handful of specially trained LAPD officers, D.A.R.E. began teaching fifth- and sixth-graders a 17-week anti-drug curriculum created by L.A. school district educators. In an interactive classroom setting, students learned about illegal drugs and alcohol and developed the practical skills necessary to resist unwanted peer pressure. Most importantly, kids learned how to build and maintain self-esteem. Within months, school districts and law enforcement agencies throughout the country began requesting the D.A.R.E. curriculum for their communities.

D.A.R.E. America, a non-profit organization, provides training, curriculum and education materials at no cost. D.A.R.E.'s middle and high school curriculum provides anti-drug education throughout a child's school years and positively impacts more than 35 million students each year in all 50 states and 44 countries. The Bureau of Justice Assistance supports its regional training centers, and over 40 states provide D.A.R.E. parent training with support from the private sector.

Since its inception, the D.A.R.E. curriculum has been revised and enhanced to address the changing needs of young people. But its method remains the same: Don't just lecture kids by saying "drugs are bad," provide students with credible instructors and the tools they need to understand and resist the societal and peer pressures that lead to drugs, alcohol, violence and gangs.

D.A.R.E.'s success is supported by dozens of local reports and studies. In a nationwide Gallup survey of D.A.R.E. graduates, more than 90% said they felt the program had helped them avoid drugs and alcohol, increased their self-confidence and enabled them to deal effectively with peer pressure. About 94% of students surveyed said that they had used one or two avoidance techniques taught by D.A.R.E. when asked by peers to do something they didn't want to do. Ninety-three percent said they have never tried marijuana, cocaine, heroin, crack or inhalants. Importantly, nine in 10 believe drug use is very dangerous. . . .

PROOF THAT D.A.R.E. WORKS

D.A.R.E. (Drug Abuse Resistance Education) has become the most widely adopted substance abuse prevention education program in the U.S. today. A statewide evaluation of D.A.R.E. in Ohio was conducted in the Spring of 1995 among 3,150 11th graders from 34 schools. . . .

D.A.R.E. 11th graders showed higher resistance to peer encouragement to use drugs than non-D.A.R.E. 11th graders. For example, D.A.R.E. students were more likely to score higher on a scale that measures if they had friends who would stop them from getting drunk and using various drugs. D.A.R.E. students also scored higher on a scale that indicated their ability to say no to close friends. Additionally, those who had been in D.A.R.E. were more likely to indicate that they would stop friends from using drugs.

Joseph F. Donnermeyer and G. Howard Phillips, "D.A.R.E. Works!" available from www.dare-america.com.

In North Carolina, an 18-year-old tracked down his old D.A.R.E. officer at a conference. Of four buddies he grew up with, he said he was the only one who hadn't wound up in prison—and the only one who had gone through the D.A.R.E. program.

To help ensure that the program continues to increase its effectiveness, D.A.R.E. America formed a Scientific Advisory Board, chaired by Dr. Herbert Kleber, to assist in evaluations and offer suggestions on future enhancements to the curriculum. Comprised of internationally recognized experts on drug prevention and research, the board met with the Department of Health and Human Services' Center for Substance Abuse Prevention to discuss the government agency's new standards for the prevention field. D.A.R.E. asked to be one of the first programs evaluated against these new standards.

While there are still 23 million drug users in this country, their average age is rising, indicating that prevention programs are having positive results with young people.

THE IMPORTANCE OF PREVENTION

No single program, no matter how successful, can combat this complex and pervasive epidemic. The solution lies in a comprehensive and coordinated, multi-faceted campaign: the combination of school and community-based prevention, enforcement, interdiction, treatment, demand-reduction programs, parental concern and increased support from both government and the private sector. We must provide our children with the knowledge and tools they need to reject drugs in the first place.

There is solid truth in the old adage "an ounce of prevention is worth a pound of cure." Just compare the $12 it costs to send a child through D.A.R.E. from kindergarten through 12th grade against the staggering amount, in excess of $238 billion, that substance abuse costs the United States each year in lost productivity, premature deaths, crime, fatal traffic and industrial accidents, incarceration, AIDS, addicted newborns, fetal alcohol syndrome, health costs, as well as factoring in the human suffering caused by drug abuse. It's clear to see that prevention efforts like D.A.R.E. make sense.

"Students who get [Drug Abuse Resistance Education] training are just as likely to use drugs as those who do not."

DRUG EDUCATION DOES NOT DISCOURAGE ADOLESCENT DRUG ABUSE

Katherine Kersten

Katherine Kersten, a staff writer for the *Minneapolis-St. Paul Star Tribune*, maintains in the following viewpoint that Drug Abuse Resistance Education (DARE), a nationwide drug education program, has done nothing to decrease teenage drug use. In fact, contends Kersten, some studies show that DARE students are more likely than others to use drugs.

As you read, consider the following questions:
1. Why is DARE ineffective, according to the author's son?
2. According to Kersten, what did the Minnesota Attorney General's Office conclude about the effectiveness of the DARE program?
3. What is the most effective deterrent against teenage drug and alcohol abuse, in Kersten's opinion?

For years, I'd seen the eye-catching, red-and-black bumper stickers: "D.A.R.E. to Keep Kids Off Drugs." I'd heard parents talk approvingly of DARE or Drug Abuse Resistance Education—the centerpiece of which is an 18-class course about drug and alcohol abuse, taught by uniformed police to fifth- or sixth-graders. So when my own son began the DARE program several years ago, I expected good things to result.

I was wholly unprepared for his reaction. "You know, Mom," he confided, several weeks into the program, "I don't think DARE works. It sounds weird, but in a way it kind of makes you want to try drugs, to see what they're like."

Incredulous, I pressed him to explain. "I'd never do it," he re-assured me. "But I guess DARE makes you curious, 'cause it tells about all kinds of things you've never thought about before. You hear lots of stories about older kids who think drugs and alcohol are fun, and you wonder why."

"But surely you're learning how to resist people who try to get you to use drugs!" I protested. "Oh," he responded, "you'd never really use that 'resistance' stuff. With bad kids you'd be scared, and with your friends you'd be afraid they'd stop liking you."

DARE is far and away the nation's most popular drug education program. Started in 1983 in Los Angeles, DARE is now used in nearly 75 percent of the nation's school systems. The program carries a huge national price tag—about $750 million annually, mostly footed by taxpayers.

Yet despite DARE's widespread use, teenage drug use has risen dramatically in recent years. Indeed, according to one study, the number of eighth-graders trying any illicit drug has nearly doubled, to 21 percent in 1995 from 11 percent in 1991.

DARE DOES NOT DETER DRUG ABUSE

The fact is, study after study has demonstrated that DARE doesn't seem to work. Students who get DARE training are just as likely to use drugs as those who do not.

For example, in 1994, a review of major DARE studies "did not find any support for a [statistically significant] impact on drug use, and [showed] DARE has no effect at all on marijuana use." In 1996, Dr. Richard Clayton—author of the most rigorous long-term study to date—wrote, "Although the results from various studies differ somewhat, all studies are consistent in finding that DARE does not have long-term effects on drug use."

Some DARE studies even reveal the dreaded "boomerang effect." One analysis found that DARE grads were more likely than others to have used marijuana recently; another, that they were significantly more likely to report inhalant use. (DARE advocates claim such critiques are obsolete, because DARE was revamped in 1994. But researchers familiar with the changes dismiss them as superficial.)

D.A.R.E. DOESN'T WORK

Despite urgent warnings from the medical community, the media and social researchers, the Drug Abuse Resistance Education program is still believed to be an effective tool in steering our nation's youth away from drug, alcohol and tobacco use. What is wrong with the D.A.R.E. program? In the simple words of Cornell University doctor and syndicated talk show host Dean Edell, "It ain't working.". . .

His statement is supported by more than 10 independent studies done on the D.A.R.E. program. Each study strongly supports the fact that students who go through D.A.R.E. are just as likely to use drugs, alcohol and tobacco as students who never step foot in a D.A.R.E. classroom. . . . The only studies that indicate D.A.R.E. is effective are studies done by D.A.R.E.

Chris Brophy, *Western Michigan University Herald*, February 23, 1998.

The Minnesota Attorney General's Office has joined the growing debate about DARE's effectiveness. On July 23, 1997, it released a 96-page report evaluating DARE's performance in Minnesota.

RESEARCH FINDINGS ON DARE

The report emphasizes that DARE is extraordinarily popular among Minnesota parents and educators. But it echoes national findings about the program's lack of success in keeping kids off drugs. Specifically:
- "The majority of DARE evaluation studies report minimal effects on the objective of preventing the onset or continued use of alcohol or other drugs."
- "There is general concern that the preventive effects of DARE are not long-lasting."
- "A large number of DARE graduates recall DARE positively and remember specific peer resistance skills taught in the program, but also report not using these skills in real-life circumstances."
- "Many students who have completed DARE question the effectiveness of the program and minimize its impact on their own behavior."

These are devastating findings. Nevertheless, Attorney General Hubert Humphrey III insists that DARE remains a "critical piece of the prevention puzzle." The report issued by his office recommends "restating the program's goals" to reflect its success in improving relationships between police and students. And it urges a variety of changes—from up-dating "role plays," to integrating DARE with other prevention programs. Realistically, however, so long as the costly and time-consuming DARE program remains entrenched in our schools, we are unlikely to have a chance to experiment with other, potentially more promising prevention programs.

One such program is Life Skills Training, developed by Gilbert Botvin, director of the Institute for Prevention Research at Cornell University Medical School. According to the *New York Times*, Life Skills Training has undergone 10 rigorous evaluations, the largest involving 4,466 seventh-graders who were followed until the end of high school. Behavioral changes initiated by the program lasted the entire six years, and use of cigarettes, alcohol and marijuana by program participants was half that of similar teens who had not had the program.

THE BEST INSURANCE AGAINST SUBSTANCE ABUSE

Until prevention programs like Life Skills Training are more widely used and studied, we can't be sure of their value. But common sense tells us that the best insurance against drug and alcohol abuse is not a "program" at all—it is a strong and close-knit family. The massive National Longitudinal Study on Adolescent Health recently confirmed this. Teen respondents who said they felt close to their families were the least likely to engage in "risky" behaviors, from drug use to sex.

Remarkably, 88 percent of Minnesotans surveyed for the Attorney General's report insisted they would support DARE even if there is no scientific evidence that it works. Why? DARE's promise of an easy, painless solution to the scourge of teenage drug abuse seems to be "an offer we can't refuse."

Our uncritical embrace of DARE exemplifies a phenomenon all too common in contemporary America. Increasingly, we try to delegate to government agencies—schools, social workers, police—responsibilities that only a family can perform effectively. If we wish to reverse teenage drug use, we must turn our attention to the "prevention program" that begins at birth. The key is not a policeman in the classroom. It is a family gathered together—night after night—around the dinner table.

| "Workplace drug tests can help to cure more than two-thirds of America's drug abusers."

EMPLOYEE DRUG TESTING REDUCES DRUG ABUSE

Ira A. Lipman

In the following viewpoint, Ira A. Lipman argues in favor of employee drug testing. Because most drug abusers are members of the workforce, he contends, employee drug testing significantly reduces drug abuse by making employment contingent upon abstinence from drugs. Furthermore, notes Lipman, the majority of employers and employees support drug-testing programs. Lipman is chairman of the board and president of Guardsmark, a private security firm in New York.

As you read, consider the following questions:
1. According to Lipman, what are the workplace costs of employee drug abuse?
2. What are the characteristics of an optimum drug-testing program, in the author's opinion?
3. In Lipman's view, what are the risks of "for cause" testing?

Drug tests on the job are nothing new. In January 1987, 21% of the corporate members of the American Management Association had such a program. With AMA members employing approximately 25% of all workers, such programs are common in Corporate America. It is now time for all businesses to realize that no company is too small to feel the harmful effects of substance abuse or benefit from testing employees for it.

The main reason for the increasing popularity of these programs is one of basic economics—drug abuse simply is too expensive a problem for businesses to ignore. Estimated costs can run as much as $60,000,000,000 a year, according to the Substance Abuse and Mental Health Services Administration (SAMHSA). The Institute for a Drug-Free Workplace reports that nearly one-half of executives and high government officials polled placed the expense of drug abuse to their organizations as high as 10% of their annual payrolls.

THE CONSEQUENCES OF EMPLOYEE DRUG ABUSE

A typical "recreational" drug user in today's workforce is 2.2 times more likely to request early dismissal or time off; 2.5 times more likely to have absences of eight days or more; three times more likely to be late for work; 3.6 times more likely to be injured or to injure another person in a workplace accident; five times more likely to be involved in an accident off the job, thus affecting attendance and performance on the job; five times more likely to file a worker's compensation claim; seven times more likely to have wage garnishments; and one-third less productive. To these measurable costs are added indirect losses associated with reduced quality of goods and services, low morale, impaired judgment, pilferage, turnover, recruitment and training expenses, employee friction, and diverted supervisory time. In short, drug abuse in the workplace seriously erodes a company's financial standing and reduces its ability to compete in the national and global arenas.

Increasing concerns about the need to work in a safe environment have led employees to become some of the strongest supporters of drug testing. A national study commissioned by the Institute for a Drug-Free Workplace found that 97% of the workers polled believed that drug testing is appropriate and "should be done under at least some circumstances," while 26% considered it a necessity. More than 90% supported the testing of airline pilots, those in safety-sensitive jobs, transportation workers, and truck drivers; about three-quarters also favored testing of other occupational areas ranging from health care to general office work.

Support for drug testing is bolstered by the fact that such programs are effective means of fighting substance abuse. In many companies, employers and employees have committed themselves to cooperating to create a drug-free workplace and to help many individuals rid themselves of addictions. As Robert L. DuPont, president of the Maryland-based Institute for Behavior and Health and clinical professor of psychology at Georgetown University School of Medicine, indicates, "The only users who have recovered from their addiction, in my experience, have recovered because someone else cared enough about them to insist that they become drug-free." With an eye on the welfare of their institutions as well as the well-being of their workforce, employers are in a perfect position to care. "I have seen hundreds of drug abusers who have recovered control of their lives because their employers put their employment on the line," DuPont notes.

Other experts agree. "The workplace is perhaps the most effective place to reach people and change their lifestyles," says William F. Current, executive director, The American Council for Drug Education. "Through drug testing and drug education in the workplace, we can create not only drug-free workplaces, but drug-free communities and drug-free families as well."

Recent reductions in the number of American workers testing positive for drug use seem to support the experts' opinions on the effectiveness of such programs. According to SmithKline Beecham Laboratories, which conducts and tabulates workplace drug tests, 18% of workers tested positive for drugs in 1987. By 1992, the number had dropped to about nine percent. While other factors contributed to this reduction, workplace testing does play a key role in lessening drug use, experts maintain.

Many employers have become advocates of drug testing for its associated advantages, such as the reduced cost of health care coverage. Drug-free employees tend to be healthier and thus make fewer claims on company insurance plans.

THE ADVANTAGES OF WORKPLACE DRUG TESTS

While implementation of a drug-testing program initially may reduce the pool of job applicants, regular pre-employment testing ultimately will help an organization attract a higher caliber of employee, ensure a safer workplace, and facilitate the delivery of better quality products and service. A Florida company that posted its policy of requiring all applicants to be drug tested saw its number of walk-in applicants plummet by 50%. A video camera mounted outside the entrance to its employment office showed why: Potential applicants would walk up to the building, read the sign, and leave.

Aren't most substance abusers unemployed? The answer is "no." While many hard-core abusers do not and perhaps can not work because of their addiction, there is ample evidence that most do hold jobs. In a 1993 survey of households, SAMHSA estimated that 70% of illegal drug users are employed and that 95% of companies nationwide report drug problems among their workers.

THE WORKPLACE COSTS OF SUBSTANCE ABUSE

Substance abuse in the workplace costs American businesses many billions of dollars a year. While there is some disagreement as to exactly how much substance abuse costs employers, there is virtually no disagreement that this cost is enormous.

Why is substance abuse so costly to employers? Substance abuse has a direct correlation to workplace accidents. In addition to the human costs associated with these accidents, employers with substance-abusing employees experience increased workers' compensation and health care costs. Moreover, substance abuse in the workplace has a demonstrated and substantial adverse impact on employee productivity and morale. . . .

Numerous studies and individual corporate experiences alike confirm that efforts to reduce substance abuse in the workplace can be extraordinarily effective. The prevalence of drug testing throughout the employer community alone demonstrates that companies recognize that their programs work. In 1997, more than 40 million drug tests were performed in the American workplace—a 1000% increase in the past 10 years.

Murray I. Lappe, Congressional Testimony, June 5, 1998.

Such statistics suggest that workplace drug tests can help to cure more than two-thirds of America's drug abusers. We at Guardsmark speak from experience. We don't sell drug-testing services at our company, but we do have drug testing for 100% of our employees and applicants—myself included. We also are 100% drug free. Such a status is rare among companies of any size or kind, but our achievement proves that workforces that are 100% drug tested and drug free are within reach.

How Drug Testing Works

The testing system at Guardsmark is a 10-panel one, meaning it screens for the presence of 10 different drugs. These include amphetamine and methamphetamine; barbiturate; benzodiazepine;

marijuana; cocaine; methadone; methaqualone; codeine and morphine; phencyclidine hydrochloride (PCP); and propoxyphene hydrochloride. While some of these have legitimate medical uses, many also carry a high potential for abuse and dependence.

The tests are conducted by laboratories approved by SAMHSA—an essential criterion for reliable results. Such labs have stringent requirements for guaranteeing the chain of custody for any specimen to prevent switching or contamination; for example, the testing company must be able to document the identities of all the technicians who handle the specimen during the drug-testing process. All positive results are verified by means of gas chromatography/mass spectrometry, the most sophisticated confirmation method available. Such safeguards make faulty test results virtually impossible.

An optimum drug-testing program should be mandatory, universal, and random. Everyone in the organization must consent to be tested and made aware that compliance is a condition of employment. If a company adopts a mandatory program, unless prohibited by law, employees can not refuse to be tested and keep their jobs.

UNIVERSAL TESTING IS BEST

A plan that is universal in scope means that, where not prohibited by law, drug tests can be administered to all applicants and current employees. Even one worker who abuses drugs can wreak havoc on an organization. Universal testing also is a response to the realization that, as soon as one attempts to define which categories of employees should be tested, it becomes clear that it is not possible to specify who is a safety risk and who is not. A secretary under the influence can cause as much damage as a drug-using dock worker. An addicted kitchen worker can be as dangerous as an addicted hospital orderly.

Because there is no way to draw the testing line with certainty, the best method for companies to achieve a drug-free workforce is to include everyone in the pool of those who are to be tested. Universal testing generally is acceptable to employees because it is perceived as fair, since it is designed to apply equally to everyone in the organization. Participation by top management is a critical feature, teaching by example the importance of the program and helping to foster acceptance and compliance at all staff levels. Employees of a large Texas-based manufacturer of advanced technological equipment told their supervisors that they didn't mind being tested so long as their bosses were tested first.

Random Drug Tests

Finally, under a random program, repeat tests can be conducted without warning on a continuing basis. A significant benefit of random testing is its deterrent value. Just as a company's announced policy of universal testing limits applications by those who use drugs, a set policy of random follow-ups can dissuade employees who might be tempted to do so after clearing the hurdle of the pre-employment drug screen.

Experts believe such a practice could have helped avert the August 1991 crash of a New York City subway train in which five people were killed and 170 others injured. Investigators found an empty crack vial in the motorman's cab on the train, and, when he was apprehended four hours later, he was drunk. At the time of the crash, the New York City Transit Authority conducted periodic drug tests of its employees, but not unannounced, random ones. The crash changed the testing policy of the city and the Federal government. New York instituted random drug and alcohol testing for city transit workers, and the U.S. Department of Transportation added alcohol testing to its earlier drug testing requirement for all transportation workers in safety-sensitive jobs.

Random testing is effective, but it must be introduced carefully. Companies that choose to adopt such a practice must first address the contractual, financial, and educational issues surrounding it. Especially important is reassuring employees who use prescription medication that the purpose of the random drug screen is not to determine legitimate use, but to detect abuse.

"For-Cause" Testing

Some firms consider the use of "for-cause" testing as a follow-up program. For-cause tests usually are administered on an as-needed basis when a supervisor has reason to suspect substance abuse by an employee. They can be helpful as a supplement to a program of random testing, but have limitations when used as the sole follow-up procedure. One is that for-cause testing bears the stigma of accusation. Another is that even experts say that they can not be certain when an employee is impaired. While such unacceptable or suspect behavior as irritability, chronic fatigue, argumentativeness, or tardiness might be drug related, it as easily might result from other factors in employees' lives. Furthermore, for-cause testing can be based too easily on supervisor bias towards race, age, sex, appearance, or job category.

While inappropriate testing can lead to employee harassment, fear of being charged with employee harassment can lead supervisors to overlook problems. For-cause testing is reactive instead of proactive. If supervisors have to wait until they see a smoking gun to require a drug screen, significant damage is likely to have occurred already. Finally, for-cause testing may lose the aura of fairness and, consequently, may not be tolerated as readily by workers. For these reasons, it is not as effective as random testing.

With approximately 8,500 employees and varying numbers of job applicants, Guardsmark spends several hundred thousand dollars each year on a drug-testing program. We are convinced the money spent is worth it, weighed against the costs of lost productivity, absenteeism, worker compensation payments, and other drug-related expenses.

"It is unfair to force workers who are not even suspected of using drugs, and whose job performance is satisfactory, to 'prove' their innocence through a degrading and uncertain procedure that violates personal privacy."

EMPLOYEE DRUG TESTING IS UNCONSTITUTIONAL AND INEFFECTIVE

American Civil Liberties Union

In the following viewpoint, the American Civil Liberties Union (ACLU) maintains that employee drug tests violate employees' right to privacy and are unreliable at detecting drug use. In the organization's view, job performance, not drug testing, should be the sole measure by which employers determine whether employees are abusing drugs. The ACLU is a national organization that works to defend the civil rights guaranteed by the U.S. Constitution.

As you read, consider the following questions:

1. According to the ACLU, why are the results of drug tests unreliable?
2. In the ACLU's opinion, why are employee drugs tests "un-American"?
3. What does the ACLU cite as effective alternatives to drug testing?

Reprinted from the ACLU Briefing Paper, "Drug Testing in the Workplace," 1996, courtesy of the American Civil Liberties Union, 1998. For archival purposes only. This document is out of print.

There was a time in the United States when your business was also your boss's business. At the turn of the century, company snooping was pervasive and privacy almost nonexistent. Your boss had the right to know who you lived with, what you drank, whether you went to church, or to what political groups you belonged. With the growth of the trade union movement and heightened awareness of the importance of individual rights, American workers came to insist that life off the job was their private affair not to be scrutinized by employers.

But major chinks have begun to appear in the wall that has separated life on and off the job, largely due to the advent of new technologies that make it possible for employers to monitor their employees' off-duty activities. Today, millions of American workers every year, in both the public and private sectors, are subjected to urinalysis drug tests as a condition for getting or keeping a job.

AN UNFAIR AND UNNECESSARY PROCESS

The American Civil Liberties Union (ACLU) opposes indiscriminate urine testing because the process is both unfair and unnecessary. It is unfair to force workers who are not even suspected of using drugs, and whose job performance is satisfactory, to "prove" their innocence through a degrading and uncertain procedure that violates personal privacy. Such tests are unnecessary because they cannot detect impairment and, thus, in no way enhance an employer's ability to evaluate or predict job performance.

Here are the ACLU's answers to some questions frequently asked by the public about drug testing in the workplace.

Q: *Don't employers have the right to expect their employees not to be high on drugs on the job?*

A: Of course they do. Employers have the right to expect their employees not to be high, stoned, drunk, or asleep. Job performance is the bottom line: If you cannot do the work, employers have a legitimate reason for firing you. But urine tests do not measure job performance. Even a confirmed "positive" provides no evidence of present intoxication or impairment; it merely indicates that a person may have taken a drug at some time in the past.

FACTS ABOUT URINE TESTS

Q: *Can urine tests determine precisely when a particular drug was used?*

A: No. Urine tests cannot determine when a drug was used. They can only detect the "metabolites," or inactive leftover traces of previously ingested substances. For example, an employee who smokes marijuana on a Saturday night may test positive the following Wednesday, long after the drug has ceased to have any effect. In that case, what the employee did on Saturday has nothing to do with his or her fitness to work on Wednesday. At the same time, a worker can snort cocaine on the way to work and test negative that same morning. That is because the cocaine has not yet been metabolized and will, therefore, not show up in the person's urine.

Q: *If you don't use drugs, you have nothing to hide—so why object to testing?*

A: Innocent people do have something to hide: their private life. The "right to be left alone" is, in the words of the late Supreme Court Justice Louis Brandeis, "the most comprehensive of rights and the right most valued by civilized men."

Analysis of a person's urine can disclose many details about that person's private life other than drug use. It can tell an employer whether an employee or job applicant is being treated for a heart condition, depression, epilepsy or diabetes. It can also reveal whether an employee is pregnant.

Q: *Are drug tests reliable?*

A: No, the drug screens used by most companies are not reliable. These tests yield false positive results at least 10 percent, and possibly as much as 30 percent, of the time. Experts concede that the tests are unreliable. At a recent conference, 120 forensic scientists, including some who worked for manufacturers of drug tests, were asked, "Is there anybody who would submit urine for drug testing if his career, reputation, freedom or livelihood depended on it?" Not a single hand was raised.

Although more accurate tests are available, they are expensive and infrequently used. And even the more accurate tests can yield inaccurate results due to laboratory error. A survey by the National Institute of Drug Abuse, a government agency, found that 20 percent of the labs surveyed mistakenly reported the presence of illegal drugs in drug-free urine samples. Unreliability also stems from the tendency of drug screens to confuse similar chemical compounds. For example, codeine and Vicks Formula 44-M have been known to produce positive results for heroin, Advil for marijuana, and Nyquil for amphetamines.

UNIVERSAL TESTING IS UN-AMERICAN

Q: *Still, isn't universal testing the best way to catch drug users?*

A: Such testing may be the easiest way to identify drug users, but it is also by far the most un-American. Americans have traditionally believed that general searches of innocent people are unfair. This tradition began in colonial times, when King George's soldiers searched everyone indiscriminately in order to uncover those few people who were committing offenses against the Crown. Early Americans deeply hated these general searches, which were a leading cause of the Revolution.

After the Revolution, when memories of the experience with warrantless searches were still fresh, the Fourth Amendment was adopted. It says that the government cannot search everyone to find the few who might be guilty of an offense. The government must have good reason to suspect a particular person before subjecting him or her to intrusive body searches. These long-standing principles of fairness should also apply to the private sector, even though the Fourth Amendment only applies to government action.

Clay Bennett/North American Syndicate. Reprinted with permission.

Urine tests are body searches, and they are an unprecedented invasion of privacy. The standard practice, in administering such tests, is to require employees to urinate in the presence of a witness to guard against specimen tampering. In the words of one judge, that is "an experience which even if courteously supervised can be humiliating and degrading." Noted a federal judge, as he invalidated a drug-testing program for municipal fire-fighters, "Drug testing is a form of surveillance, albeit a technological one."

Q: But shouldn't exceptions be made for certain workers, such as airline pilots, who are responsible for the lives of others?

A: Obviously, people who are responsible for others' lives should be held to high standards of job performance. But urine testing will not help employers do that because it does not detect impairment.

If employers in transportation and other industries are really concerned about the public's safety, they should abandon imperfect urine testing and test performance instead. Computer-assisted performance tests already exist and, in fact, have been used by NASA for years on astronauts and test pilots. These tests can actually measure hand-eye coordination and response time, do not invade people's privacy, and can improve safety far better than drug tests can.

THE ROLE OF EDUCATION AND VOLUNTARY REHABILITATION

Q: Drug use costs industry millions in lost worker productivity each year. Don't employers have a right to test as a way of protecting their investment?

A: Actually, there are no clear estimates about the economic costs to industry resulting from drug use by workers. Proponents of drug testing claim the costs are high, but they have been hard pressed to translate that claim into real figures. And some who make such claims are manufacturers of drug tests, who obviously stand to profit from industry-wide urinalysis. In any event, employers have better ways to maintain high productivity, as well as to identify and help employees with drug problems. Competent supervision, professional counseling and voluntary rehabilitation programs may not be as simple as a drug test, but they are a better investment in America.

Our nation's experience with cigarette smoking is a good example of what education and voluntary rehabilitation can accomplish. Since 1965, the proportion of Americans who smoke cigarettes has gone down from 43 percent to 32 percent. This dramatic decrease was a consequence of public education and the availability of treatment on demand. Unfortunately, instead of adequately funding drug clinics and educational programs, the government has cut these services so that substance abusers sometimes have to wait for months before receiving treatment.

A VIOLATION OF THE CONSTITUTION

Q: Have any courts ruled that mandatory urine testing of government employees is a violation of the Constitution?

A: Yes. Many state and federal courts have ruled that testing programs in public workplaces are unconstitutional if they are not based on some kind of individualized suspicion. Throughout the country, courts have struck down programs that randomly tested police officers, fire-fighters, teachers, civilian army employees, prison guards and employees of many federal agencies. The ACLU and public employee unions have represented most of these victorious workers.

In Washington, D.C., for example, one federal judge had this to say about a random drug testing program that would affect thousands of government employees: "This case presents for judicial consideration a wholesale deprivation of the most fundamental privacy rights of thousands upon thousands of loyal, law-abiding citizens...."

In 1989, for the first time, the U.S. Supreme Court ruled on the constitutionality of testing government employees not actually suspected of drug use. In two cases involving U.S. Customs guards and railroad workers, the majority of the Court held that urine tests are searches, but that these particular employees could be tested without being suspected drug users on the grounds that their Fourth Amendment right to privacy was outweighed by the government's interest in maintaining a drug-free workplace.

Although these decisions represent a serious setback, the Court's ruling does not affect all government workers, and the fight over the constitutionality of testing is far from over.

UPHOLDING THE RIGHT TO PRIVACY

Q: If the Constitution can't help them, how can private employees protect themselves against drug testing?

A: Court challenges to drug testing programs in private workplaces are underway throughout the country. These lawsuits involve state constitutional and statutory laws rather than federal constitutional law. Some are based on common law actions that charge specific, intentional injuries; others are breach of contract claims. Some have been successful, while others have failed. Traditionally, employers in the private sector have extremely broad discretion in personnel matters.

In most states, private sector employees have virtually no protection against drug testing's intrusion on their privacy, unless they belong to a union that has negotiated the prohibition or restriction of workplace testing. One exception to this bleak picture is California, in which the state constitution specifies a right to privacy that applies, not only to government action, but to actions by private business as well.

In addition to California, seven states have enacted protective legislation that restricts drug testing in the private workplace and gives employees some measure of protection from unfair and unreliable testing: Montana, Iowa, Vermont and Rhode Island have banned all random or blanket drug testing of employees (that is, testing without probable cause or reasonable suspicion), and Minnesota, Maine and Connecticut permit random testing only of employees in "safety sensitive" positions. The laws in these states also mandate confirmatory testing, use of certified laboratories, confidentiality of test results and other procedural protections. While they are not perfect, these new laws place significant limits on employers' otherwise unfettered authority to test and give employees the power to resist unwarranted invasions of privacy.

The ACLU will continue to press other states to pass similar statutes and to lobby the U.S. Congress to do the same.

> "Independent research conducted by Johns Hopkins, Michigan and New York universities tells us anti-drug advertising can effectively 'unsell' drugs to children."

AD CAMPAIGNS WILL DETER TEENAGE DRUG ABUSE

Brad Owen

In 1998, the government instituted the National Youth Anti-Drug Media Campaign, a five-year media campaign aimed at preventing adolescent drug abuse through antidrug advertisements. Brad Owen, arguing in favor of the government media campaign, contends in the following viewpoint that advertising has the power to change teens' attitudes about drugs. Owen writes for the *Columbian*, a newspaper based in southern Washington.

As you read, consider the following questions:
1. What proof of the effectiveness of advertising does Owen provide?
2. According to the author, how will the new antidrug media campaign redefine the media's obligation to public service?
3. How did attitudes about drug use change from the late 1980s to the early 1990s, in Owen's view?

Reprinted from Brad Owen, "Put Ads to Work 'Unselling' Drugs to Kids," *The Columbian*, July 27, 1997, by permission of the author.

Adolescent drug use is on the rise in America and at an even faster rate in Washington, and Congress can do something about it.

Sitting before the U.S. House and Senate is one of the most intelligent anti-drug proposals to come along in a very long time. The idea calls for using 1 percent of the $16 billion federal drug budget—or $175 million—to buy prime-time media exposure for powerful, hard-hitting anti-drug ads targeting children, teen-agers and parents. For the first time we would have, in part, our national anti-drug campaign run much like a commercial advertising effort. [In 1998, Congress appropriated $195 million for the first year of a five-year National Youth Anti-Drug Media Campaign.]

The Partnership for a Drug-Free America has run a national anti-drug ad campaign since 1987, but has done so totally dependent on media companies running ads for free. During the 1980s, this approach worked, but it can't today. The splintering of the media—the creation of new television networks and hundreds of cable channels—has created intense competition for ratings and survival in the media industry. Market forces are squeezing public service announcements off the air, and support for public service simply will not return to levels required for effectiveness.

Today children spend as many hours each week watching television as they do in a classroom. Why not use this tremendously influential tool to fight drugs?

ADVERTISING WORKS

Advertising, we know, works. Politicians use it to get elected; the U.S. Army uses it to recruit soldiers; and corporations invest billions in advertising each year. McDonald's spends $599 million annually to bring people to its golden arches. Kellogg's invests $368 million each year to sell breakfast foods. And Nike spends $191 million, mostly on television air time, to peddle Air Jordans.

Independent research conducted by Johns Hopkins, Michigan and New York universities tells us anti-drug advertising can effectively "unsell" drugs to children. Drug experts believe that these ads contributed to declines in drug use in the '80s, when they ran heavily. Today prime-time slots are just too lucrative to give away, but they offer just the type of exposure needed to effectively reach children.

While acknowledging economic realities, the media campaign doesn't ignore the media's obligation to public service—it redefines it. For every federal dollar spent, media companies will be asked to match purchased advertising with donations of support, putting this effort—with $350 million in media exposure—on par with the Coca-Colas, AT&Ts and IBMs of the world. The reach of this campaign would produce real changes in drug-related attitudes among children.

HELPING TEENS REJECT DRUGS

Attitudes are, of course, what drive behavior. During the late '80s, a consistent barrage of anti-drug information via news, entertainment and advertising helped a generation of Americans reject once-fashionable drugs. Among this group, cocaine use is down by 75 percent, overall drug use by 50 percent.

USING THE MEDIA TO FIGHT DRUG ABUSE

On average, American children are exposed to media at least eight hours per day through television, radio, movies, recorded music, comics, and video games. The messages that society sends young people about illegal drugs (as well as alcohol and tobacco) are frequently contradictory. Both media programming and advertising content tend to portray substance use as common and normal. For example, by his or her eighteenth birthday, an average adolescent will have seen 100,000 television commercials for beer and will have watched 65,000 scenes on television depicting beer drinking. Although popular media depict illicit substances less frequently than alcohol and tobacco, those depictions often portray illicit substance use as acceptable and "cool." At the same time, anti-drug messages in the media are dwindling. Free time and space for drug-prevention public service messages are at a ten-year low. . . .

Fortunately, the growing awareness of America's parents and the bipartisan commitment of the U.S. Congress have produced an important response to the drug dangers facing our youth. In 1998, Congress appropriated $195 million for the first year of a five-year National Youth Anti-Drug Media Campaign. We are about to undertake a multi-faceted communication campaign that can "de-normalize" drug use in the minds of youth and empower parents to help children with this critical problem.

Barry R. McCaffrey, *Vital Speeches of the Day*, August 1, 1998.

Teen-agers in the early 1990s, however, were not so fortunate. As public attention turned away from drugs and toward the Persian Gulf and other issues in 1990–91, the anti-drug drumbeat of the '80s was replaced by marijuana leaves on shirts and caps worn by teen-agers; a retro '60s fashion craze bringing back bell-bottoms and nostalgia for pot; musicians dedicating CDs to smoking marijuana, blunts and legalization; and drugs once again appearing on television as playful, fun things to do.

Since 1991, teen drug use has doubled—and in some age categories tripled—with no end in sight. The media campaign would support the critically important work of each and every local prevention, education and treatment program in Washington and all across America. That's why Washington State Community Mobilization and its local affiliates along with the Community Anti-Drug Coalitions of America—representing some 4,000 grass-roots organizations—support the anti-drug campaign.

Importantly, the Partnership for a Drug-Free America . . . will offer its inventory of more than 200 anti-drug ads—valued at $50 million—to this program for free.

The potential return on this investment—cutting demand for drugs among children—is enormous. Advertising can create demand for products and services, and it can reduce demand as well. If McDonald's is willing to spend $600 million each year to sell cheeseburgers, shouldn't the country put the power of advertising to work to unsell drugs to children?

> "No amount of advertising is likely to stop a young person . . . from turning to drugs."

AD CAMPAIGNS WILL NOT DETER TEENAGE DRUG ABUSE

Ryan H. Sager

The National Youth Anti-Drug Media Campaign, a government program instituted in 1998, seeks to combat teenage drug use through television advertising. In the following viewpoint, Ryan H. Sager argues that media campaigns and other government programs do not deter teenage drug abuse because they fail to address the reasons teens turn to drugs. Sager is a college student and former intern of the Cato Institute, a public policy research foundation whose goal is to limit the role of government and protect individual freedoms.

As you read, consider the following questions:
1. According to Sager, how do teens view anti-drug advertisements?
2. Why do teenagers turn to drugs, in the author's opinion?
3. In Sager's view, what keeps young people from using drugs?

Reprinted from Ryan H. Sager, "Drug Lure That the Ads Can't Cure," *The Washington Times*, August 8, 1998, by permission of *The Washington Times*.

On Thursday, July 9, 1998, President Bill Clinton launched the latest offensive in this country's War on Drugs. Presenting a bipartisan front, the president stood alongside Republican House Speaker Newt Gingrich to unveil a new five-year, $2 billion anti-drug ad campaign. The campaign will focus primarily on television advertising: It is intended to educate children about the dangers of drugs and to discourage their use. However, as you watch this ad campaign—which is larger than the campaigns for Sprint, American Express and Nike—you should ask yourself one vital question: Will these advertisements stop any significant number of children from using drugs?

As a teen-ager and a sophomore in college, I can tell you that the answer to that question is a resounding no.

The government has been trying to solve the drug problem for years now but has had little to show for its efforts. Even at the height of the War on Drugs in 1992, a full 32 percent of high school seniors reported having used marijuana; nearly 10 percent had used hallucinogens; and cocaine use (including crack cocaine) was in the double digits.

A Target of Teen Ridicule

Now politicians desperate to be seen as doing something about the drug problem have come up with the idea that if only we can saturate the air waves with enough anti-drug propaganda, we will finally start to see teen drug use begin to fall. However, I can tell you firsthand that such drug education initiatives have become a joke among teen-agers. Everything from D.A.R.E. [Drug Abuse Resistance Education] to drug education classes to anti-drug advertisements is a target of ridicule for youth who see those efforts as nothing more than heavy-handed admonitions from hypocritical Baby Boomers. Everyone I know has been through a drug education program of some sort and has seen anti-drug advertising, yet I do not know a single person who has stayed away from drugs because of those influences.

So, why are those programs so utterly incapable of producing results? Because they cannot strike at the root of the problem, which is moral and spiritual.

Why Teens Turn to Drugs

Some teens turn to drugs out of boredom, some out of insecurity—but most turn to drugs as an escape from lives that seem empty. As Patrick Fagan, senior policy analyst at the Heritage Foundation and a former family therapist and clinical psychologist, says, "Behind teen-age drug use is the unhappy, empty heart that quite a few of our young adolescents have. If they're not happy, and the empty heart needs filling, they turn to other things. Too often, those other things are drugs, since they give at least the feeling of security and happiness while blocking reality."

Teen-agers turn to drugs because they have not been provided with the inner resources to face life with confidence and hope. They have not been given a strong moral or spiritual foundation, and therefore they feel empty, confused and afraid.

Chris Britt. Reprinted by permission of Copley News Service.

I myself have watched a close friend with a fairly normal life go through a particularly hard semester in school and quickly turn to drugs after having been relatively happy and straight.

On the other hand, I'd have plenty of excuses for turning to drugs, should I choose to make them. My parents are divorced, and my 10-year-old brother Zachary died when I was 14. Still, I have never found it necessary to use an illicit drug.

The difference between us is that I was lucky enough to have received a strong spiritual upbringing from my mother. The knowledge that my life has meaning, regardless of how the world may look at any given moment, has given me the strength not to need drugs. Lack of such an understanding on my friend's part, I believe, allowed her to make a wrong turn.

NOT A GOVERNMENT PROBLEM

The problem of teen-age drug use in America is not a problem of education—teen-agers know the risks. No amount of advertising is likely to stop a young person inclined to do so from turning to drugs. The government has already proven itself unable to make a difference. What can make a difference is parenting. Says Mr. Fagan, "If parents have not taught their children how to find happiness, then those children are at risk for mistaking pleasure and excitement as a route to happiness."

Only if parents take the time to instill in their children moral values and spiritual teachings will they realize the power within themselves to meet all of life's challenges. I am glad my mother did that, instead of counting on the government to do her job.

| "Each dollar spent on drug treatment *7* saves Americans $7 by reducing or avoiding costs relating to criminal justice, health care, and welfare."

TREATMENT PROGRAMS HAVE BEEN PROVEN TO REDUCE DRUG ABUSE

Office of National Drug Control Policy

In the following viewpoint, the Office of National Drug Control Policy (ONDCP) contends that drug treatment programs have been shown to be highly effective in rehabilitating drug users. Furthermore, the organization claims, drug treatment programs benefit society by reducing the criminal activity and health care costs associated with drug abuse. Established by Congress in 1988, the ONDCP is a federal agency responsible for developing and coordinating the policies, goals, and objectives of the nation's program for reducing the use of illicit drugs.

As you read, consider the following questions:

1. What evidence does the ONDCP provide that drug treatment reduces criminal activity?
2. How should the criminal justice system deal with hard-core addicts, according to the organization?
3. What alternatives to prison for first time, nonviolent offenders are cited by the ONDCP?

Reprinted from the Office of Drug Control Policy's paper "Demonstrating Treatment Effectiveness," www.whitehousedrugpolicy.gov/drugfact/trteffc.html.

There are numerous studies that support the logic and rationale of providing treatment for drug users. The research reveals that the societal costs of untreated addiction (e.g. violence, crime, poor health, and family breakup) far exceed the costs of providing treatment.

A 1995 report from the U.S. Department of Health and Human Services highlighted findings of seven research projects that supported the effectiveness of drug treatment. One research effort in particular, *Evaluating Recovery Services: The California Drug and Alcohol Treatment Assessment*, clearly demonstrated the benefits of treatment as it relates to criminal activity. That study showed that the level of criminal activity declined by two-thirds as a result of drug treatment. The longer hardcore users stay in treatment, the greater the reduction in their criminal activity and in the costs associated with this activity. The same study, corroborated by other research, demonstrated that each dollar spent on drug treatment saves Americans $7 by reducing or avoiding costs relating to criminal justice, health care, and welfare.

RESEARCH SUPPORTS THE EFFECTIVENESS OF TREATMENT

Among the key findings in other treatment studies, a study by the RAND Corporation demonstrated that treatment was more effective than law enforcement as a means to reduce the demand for illicit drugs.

Another study by the National Academy of Sciences (Institute of Medicine) demonstrated that treatment was effective in reducing criminal activity and emergency room visits and in increasing rates of employment.

It is critical to remember that hardcore drug users are at the heart of the nation's drug problem. Two-thirds of the nation's supply of cocaine is consumed by about one-quarter of the total number of cocaine users. In order to get money for drugs, these hardcore users often commit crimes. In addition, hardcore drug users frequently are "vectors" for the spread of infectious diseases such as hepatitis, tuberculosis, and HIV. Tragically, hardcore drug users are often part of an intergenerational pattern of addiction.

LINKING DRUG TREATMENT AND LAW ENFORCEMENT

The adequacy of the drug treatment system is only one aspect of solving the problem of hardcore drug use. Drug treatment services must also be effectively linked with criminal justice services. Hardcore addicts must be held accountable by the criminal justice system for their illegal behavior, and they must receive support from the treatment system to change their behavior and end their drug use. Effective linkage between criminal justice and treatment systems empowers judges to use a valuable range of treatment and punishment options. The passage of Public Law 103-322, the Violent Crime Control Act of 1994, did much to foster coordination between the treatment and criminal justice systems, supporting drug courts and other nonviolent offender management programs, at the State and local levels.

THE DRAMATIC IMPACT OF DRUG TREATMENT PROGRAMS

The National Treatment Improvement Evaluation Study (NTIES) evaluated the impact of drug and alcohol treatment on 4,411 people who participated in programs funded by the Substance Abuse and Mental Health Services Administration's (SAMHSA) Center for Substance Abuse Treatment (CSAT). These programs focused on reaching underserved and vulnerable populations such as minorities, pregnant and at-risk women, youth, public housing residents, welfare recipients, and those in the criminal justice system. . . .

The new findings include:

• Among women in treatment, drug use declined by more than 40 percent for as long as a year after leaving treatment.

• Among young adults, depending on the treatment setting any drug use was reduced by 31 to 47 percent and primary drug use (the drug cited as the reason a participant entered treatment) was reduced by 23 to 45 percent.

• Among the chronic users of marijuana, treatment resulted in a 45 percent reduction in use, and for those who used marijuana in combination with other drugs a 50 percent reduction.

• Among users of cocaine and/or crack, treatment reduced cocaine use by 55 percent and reduced crack use by 51 percent.

• Among those who reported supporting themselves through criminal activity, treatment reduced illegal activity by 49 percent.

The Substance Abuse and Mental Health Services Administration, Press Release, September 17, 1997, available from http://www.ncjrs.org/nties97/nties97p.htm.

For hardcore users who have committed serious crimes, treatment must be provided during the incarceration. Although rehabilitation of a drug offender is a long-term process, rehabilitation is a logical investment because most drug offenders will eventually be returned to our communities. Effective correctional treatment includes accurate initial assessment of rehabilitative needs, appropriate programming within the correctional institution, and, most importantly, extensive transitional supervision and support as the offender is gradually reintegrated into the community.

Prison-based drug treatment has been shown to be an effective means of controlling drug use and recidivism. Intensive treatment programs, such as therapeutic communities and aftercare, are especially effective for serious offenders who are serving long-term jail and prison sentences.

ALTERNATIVES TO PRISON-BASED TREATMENT

Studies also indicate that drug courts can function as alternatives to prison and effectively coerce non-violent, first offenders into treatment. Offender management programs, such as drug courts and Treatment Alternatives to Street Crime (TASC), have linked drug-addicted individuals to appropriate forms of treatment. Progress has been made by drug court programs in Fort Lauderdale, Florida; Miami, Florida; Oakland, California; Portland, Oregon; New York City; and the District of Columbia. These programs have demonstrated that closely supervised, court-ordered rehabilitation can be successful in reducing drug use, and freeing prison space for serious and violent offenders.

Effective and timely treatment will allow the United States to intervene early in the cycle of addiction. Early intervention is critical in order to reach youths, who stand to benefit from treatment. This is also the most efficient way to conduct business. Intervention as early as possible in the drug use continuum simplifies the task of the treatment provider and makes treatment less expensive and more successful. The drug user has had less time for the more insidious effects of drug use to take hold. At this stage, criminal behaviors are less entrenched, other high-risk behaviors are less ingrained, general health is better, and recovery and rehabilitation are less problematic.

"Rehabilitators . . . tend to become angry when asked for evidence of [drug treatment] effectiveness, which wouldn't be their reaction if they had much evidence."

TREATMENT PROGRAMS HAVE NOT BEEN PROVEN TO REDUCE DRUG ABUSE

Fred Reed

Fred Reed maintains in the following viewpoint that drug treatment programs, while widely viewed as successful, have not been proven to permanently reduce drug abuse. According to Reed, existing studies that support the effectiveness of drug rehabilitation are flawed by unreliable and contradictory data. Reed is a syndicated columnist based in Washington, D.C.

As you read, consider the following questions:
1. According to Reed, why do many politicians promote rehabilitation?
2. How is the RAND drug treatment study flawed, in Reed's view?
3. In the author's opinion, why is it difficult to obtain accurate data on the effectiveness of drug treatment programs?

Reprinted from Fred Reed, "Does Drug Rehab Work? Nobody Knows," *The Metropolitan Times*, March 31, 1998, by permission of *The Washington Times*.

Are efforts at rehabilitating drug users worthwhile?

My guess is that they are not, but a guess is a poor basis for policy. We need to know. The trouble is in part that it is not easy to find reliable evaluations of rehab programs, and in part that so many people have agendas to promote.

Politicians know that nothing can be done to stop the flow of drugs into the United States. Smuggling is both too easy and too profitable for interdiction of supplies to work.

Imprisoning dealers and users doesn't work either. The jails already are bursting; and the costs, both political and financial, of building ever more cells do not permit much increase in incarceration, which quite likely wouldn't work anyway.

Politicians do not want to tell the public that nothing can be done about a problem that people regard as extremely serious. Nor do they want the heat that would come from stuffing an even larger proportion of the black population into jail.

AN EASY WAY OUT

The easiest way out is to promote rehabilitation, which sounds compassionate and constructive and doesn't antagonize influential groups. Whether it works doesn't matter too much.

For some time, I have been hearing here and there about a 1994 study by RAND, which, according to some accounts, said that every dollar spent on rehab saves $7 in spending on such things as imprisonment and law enforcement.

RAND is usually good, so I got a copy of the study. It is, in fact, not a study of rehabilitation but an attempt to compare the dollar effectiveness of increasing spending on different approaches to the cocaine epidemic—e.g., of spending more on domestic interdiction, on eradication in the source countries, and so on.

The study is murky because it relies, having no choice, on soft data and assumptions that are plausible but not necessarily correct (a problem the authors note).

Some of it seems self-contradictory: "An estimated 13 percent of heavy users treated do not return to heavy use after treatment. Although not all of these departures are permanent."

The study concludes, after warnings about the difficulty of estimating such things, that a dollar of rehab saves $7.46 in societal costs: crime, lost productivity, etc.

If so, fine. Let's rehabilitate like crazy.

THE PROBLEM WITH DRUG TREATMENT DATA

But the whole thing is so awash in approximations and extrapolations that it leaves the reader uneasy, and it doesn't square well with what I have seen in Washington, D.C.—residents of treatment programs coming out on the street to score, then going back in—or with regular assertions by cops that the city's rehab efforts are scams to make money for those who run them.

Whose data do you trust? How do you even get data?

For example, when a former addict leaves rehab, how does one even know where he is five years later, much less whether he is using? Presumably one doesn't simply call and ask. ("Oh, yeah, I'm smoking again. Come bust me for possession.")

No Evidence for the Effectiveness of Treatment

The absence of convincing evidence about the effectiveness of drug abuse treatment results from the lack of rigorous evaluations. Only a handful of randomized clinical trials have been conducted to date. More need to be done, and valid and comprehensive measures of treatment effectiveness need to be employed in these studies in order to end the reliance of treatment researchers on clients' self-reports of sensitive behaviors. Treatment research also needs more post-treatment follow-ups to show that treatment effects persist once clients leave their programs.

Finally, researchers must learn what happens to untreated drug abusers. Past and current research focuses almost exclusively on drug abusers who enter treatment. This research does not make comparisons between treated and untreated drug abusers and cannot answer the most fundamental question of all: is treatment more cost-effective than no treatment?

Robert Apsler, *American Enterprise*, March/April 1994.

It is a commonplace that Alcoholics Anonymous is effective in rehabilitating drunks. Narcotics Anonymous (NA) is said to do the same for addicts.

But if you look into these organizations, you find that they don't keep records of members (being, after all, anonymous), and don't even define "member."

Some people show up at NA for one night, others for a week or month or year. When they disappear, often no one knows whether they have gone back on drugs, moved, or quit and stayed clean. A few dedicated permanent members attribute their salvation, no doubt correctly, to NA—but the rate of success seems indeterminable.

The half-dozen publicly employed rehab counselors I have talked to have been almost evangelical in their enthusiasm, which is normal in the psychology industry—UFO-abduction therapists are equally convinced. The rehabilitators also tend to become angry when asked for evidence of effectiveness, which wouldn't be their reaction if they had much evidence.

A NEED FOR RELIABLE DATA

So . . . what are we getting for our rehab dollar? And how do we find out?

Somebody needs to put in the time to come up with reliable data. In particular, studies need control groups. How many addicts who want to be in rehab would quit by themselves? Nicotine addicts who quit usually do so on their own. How much more effective is rehab than nothing?

The answer might be surprising—to me, at any rate. Maybe it would turn out that rehab, or some particular form of rehab, actually works well, at least with certain kinds of addicts. But we need to know.

Periodical Bibliography

The following articles have been selected to supplement the diverse views presented in this chapter. Addresses are provided for periodicals not indexed in the *Readers' Guide to Periodical Literature*, the *Alternative Press Index*, the *Social Sciences Index*, or the *Index to Legal Periodicals and Books*.

Eva Bertram and Kenneth E. Sharpe	"War Ends, Drugs Win," *Nation*, January 6, 1997.
Current Biography	"McCaffrey, Barry R.," July 1997.
Current History	Special issue on narcotics, April 1998.
Don C. Des Jarlais	"Harm Reduction: A Framework for Incorporating Science into Drug Policy," *American Journal of Public Health*, January 1995.
Robert Dreyfuss	"Hawks and Doves: Who's Who in the Drug War," *Rolling Stone*, August 7, 1997.
Drug Policy Letter	"The Drug War in Black and White," special section, Winter 1996. Available from 4455 Connecticut Ave. NW, Suite B-500, Washington, DC 20008-2328.
Milton Friedman	"There's No Justice in the War on Drugs," *New York Times*, January 11, 1998.
Craig Horowitz	"The No-Win War and Its Discontents," *New York*, February 5, 1996. Available from 444 Madison Ave., New York, NY 10022-6999.
Jeremy Lennard and Steven Ambrus	"The Lost War on Drugs," *World Press Review*, February 1998.
Robert L. Maginnis	"How to Win the Drug War," *World & I*, December 1996. Available from 3600 New York Ave. NE, Washington, DC 20002.
Barry R. McCaffrey	"The Next Front in the Drug War: The Media," *Christian Science Monitor*, May 30, 1997.
Nation	"The Wrong Drug War," March 23, 1998.
Reason	"Drug Trial," March 10, 1998.
Sally L. Satel	"Opiates for the Masses," *Wall Street Journal*, June 8, 1998.

CHAPTER 3

Is U.S. Drug Policy Effective in Dealing with Drug Abuse?

CHAPTER PREFACE

Each year the Office of National Drug Control Policy (ONDCP) issues its *National Drug Control Strategy*. In 1997 the report included a new ten-year plan to reduce drug use and availability 50 percent by 2007. To meet this goal, the United States will spend roughly $17 billion each year from 1999 through 2003. The strategy's top priority goal is to reduce youth drug use. The second goal is to reduce crime through law enforcement and drug treatment for prisoners. The remaining three goals are to provide treatment for addicts, prevent drugs from entering the United States, and destroy drug-trafficking organizations and sources of supply.

Supporters of this continued war on drugs believe similar policies were responsible for the dramatic decline in drug use during the '80s and '90s—since 1992, levels of drug use have been 50 percent below the record high levels of 1979, according to the ONDCP. But the ONDCP warns that "The moment we believe ourselves victorious and drop our guard, the drug problem will resurface with the next generation." According to the *Strategy*, for example, between 1991 and 1997 funding for anti-drug public service announcements (PSAs) dropped $100 million, and teen drug use increased. ONDCP aims to reverse this trend by allocating $195 million for PSAs that will air through 2002. Because of this need for vigilance, say the authors of the *Strategy*, the term "war on drugs" is misleading: "Although wars are expected to end, drug control is a continuous challenge."

However, many critics of U.S. drug policy think the war metaphor is appropriate, and that the war is being lost. Despite a decrease in casual drug use, they point out, the number of addicts in America remains in the millions. Federal funding for drug treatment is less than half of what is spent on law enforcement and interdiction—programs that critics say have failed to curb the drug supply or reduce drug-related crime. Instead, they maintain, "casualties" in the war on drugs accumulate as more people are imprisoned because of overly harsh drug laws. The Department of Justice reports that drug offenders account for nearly three-quarters of the growth in the federal prison population, which has more than doubled since 1985.

Despite increasing criticism of the war on drugs, most Americans believe that reducing drug abuse should remain a national priority. The authors in the following chapter examine the effectiveness of these efforts.

> *"Anyone who looks objectively at America's drug war will see that it is racist, violent, corrupt and unsuccessful."*

THE WAR ON DRUGS HAS FAILED

Joseph McNamara

Joseph McNamara is a former police chief and is currently a research fellow at the Hoover Institution on War, Revolution, and Peace at Stanford University in California. The following viewpoint is adapted from a speech he gave to the Commonwealth Club of San Francisco on March 26, 1997. In it McNamara argues that the war on drugs cannot be won. Law enforcement can do little to deter drug-related crime, he says, and efforts to prevent drugs from entering the United States have almost no effect. The war on drugs is a failed policy, McNamara maintains, and claims to the contrary are merely antidrug propaganda.

As you read, consider the following questions:
1. How much land would it take to grow the entire supply of drugs for the United States, according to the author?
2. According to McNamara, what percentage of the drugs entering the United States does the government say it seizes?
3. What statistics does the author offer in support of his claim that the numbers of drug arrests are racially skewed?

Reprinted from Joseph McNamara, "The Drug War," a speech delivered to the Commonwealth Club of San Francisco, March 26, 1997, by permission of the author.

What is the principle behind the United States international war on drugs? It is a blurry picture. There is no clear line between the dangerous molecules that are made illegal and the safe molecules that we decide may be used under proper supervision. The most dangerous drugs of all are alcohol and tobacco, which kill close to a million Americans a year. If we look at all illegal drugs—cocaine, heroin, LSD, PCP—it is estimated that they kill between 3,000 and 20,000 Americans a year. It is quite clear that we are not reacting to the danger of drugs.

Why have we waged this enormously unsuccessful and costly war against drugs? About 2 centuries ago certain groups in the United States began lobbying efforts to attach a criminal and amoral stigma to drug use. They succeeded in getting drugs outlawed. How did we get into this situation?

England used to rule the world and waged two wars to force China to accept opium. The use of opium was popular in England at the time and without the stigma that it has today. So opium was sold to China and subsequently caused problems there. When the American missionaries came to China they found the effects very destructive. They began to lobby England and other countries to stop trading opium, and they began to campaign aggressively in America. The Congressional Record is quite clear. Drugs were not criminalized in part because of complaints from the police or medical authorities. They were criminalized because religious groups got their version of sin put into the penal code. In 1914 they succeeded in getting the Harrison Act passed, which is the cornerstone of the legislation in the United States.

DOOMED TO FAIL

Prior to 1914, the United States had a drug problem in the sense that many people were using drugs without being aware of the dangers. But there was no international black market, no organized crime involving drugs, none of the terrible violence and world-wide corruption that we see today. Since drugs were criminalized we have all those things. Estimates are that the per capita use of drugs is twice what it was before drugs were criminalized. I am not in favor of drug use. I think all drugs possess danger and require regulation. What I am suggesting is that we have two extremes. On one side we have the U.S. war on drugs; on the other side we have pre-1914 total market freedom for any drugs. Neither of these extremes is the answer but in between there are a lot of things that could occur.

The war on drugs cannot succeed. About $500 worth of cocaine or heroin in a source country—Mexico, Bolivia, Colombia, Peru—will bring as much as $100,000 on the streets of an American city. All the cops and prisons and armies of the world can't stop this; it is an economic force that is simply unstoppable. The profit is there because of prohibition. You all know what happened when the United States, from 1920 to 1933, prohibited alcohol. We had violence, corruption, the formation of an organized criminal structure which is still with us today. Because our thinking about these substances is frozen a century ago we are unable to rationally look at what the drug war is doing to America.

AN AMERICAN PROBLEM

The war on drugs has not reduced drug use. The United States says that it will reduce or eliminate foreign production of drugs. If you have followed the news over recent months you know that this is ludicrous. The fact is that many of these countries are poor, and drug profits are greater than their gross domestic product. During the presidential campaign, George Bush went to a summit with the presidents of Peru, Argentina, Brazil, and Colombia. They told him bluntly that they were not going to destroy their countries in a civil war because we Americans can't control our demand for drugs. That is a very legitimate point. This problem exists because millions and millions of Americans are willing to spend billions and billions of dollars to purchase something even though it is illegal, even though they have been told that it is dangerous for their health.

The entire illicit supply of drugs for the United States could probably be grown in about 50 square miles, almost anywhere in the world. With that in mind, the government's contention that they can stop foreign production of drugs is ridiculous. The government has to lie to itself. It decertifies Colombia for aid because Colombia wasn't trying hard enough to prohibit drugs, and then they increased aid. These countries hate our hypocrisy, our overbearing methods; they think this is an American problem and that we are very disrespectful of their sovereignty and indeed we are.

Strategy two was that since we can't stop production of drugs, we seize them at the border. The government estimates that they seize about 10 percent. One indication of how unsuccessful this is is that despite seizures of tons of cocaine and heroin, the street price remains stable. The supply already here is so great that even vast seizures of drugs does not cause a rise in the price. Early in the drug war, the government said that tough enforcement increased the price of drugs and made them harder to get. Those on the front lines of policing said that it didn't make it harder, but it made it more expensive and made drug users commit more crimes to get money for the drugs. That strategy of interdiction also fails because of our vast borders, the enormous volume of international trade, and what is left of the Constitution's prohibitions against unlawful search and seizure.

MASSIVE INCARCERATION

The third aspect of the government's strategy is massive incarceration. We now have 1.6 million people under penal sanction in the United States, the greatest number in our history. Many are in for long, mandatory sentences of 5, 10, 15 years in prison. Many serve 80 percent of that time. Judges increasingly do not have discretion. This imprisonment falls most heavily on minorities. There is an old racist stream that runs through drug prohibition. The Congressional Record when the missionaries were calling for making drugs illegal is quite explicit. They talked about their efforts to Christianize the "yellow heathen" and to save the "Inferior races." There was also testimony that these substances made black men rape white women. In 1937, the Marijuana Tax Act made marijuana illegal with the same racist commentary and the same inflated erroneous rhetoric that these drugs cause violence. The government's own study indicates that only 4 percent of homicides take place because someone is out of their mind on drugs. The other violence associated with drugs is the drug trade, the commerce between drug dealers, and the culture of drug dealing. Drug arrests of non-whites are four to five times greater than for whites, despite the fact that about 80 percent of drug crimes are committed by whites, and this is reflected in the prison population.

OMINOUS FUTURE

We have this ominous future before us, people doing mandatory sentences who some day will get out. What chance are they going to have in life? We have drug-free work places so nobody with a drug record could get a job to begin with. We now have drug-free housing; if your son or nephew gets busted for pot someplace else, you will be evicted from public housing. We have created this monster for ourselves; we virtually have ensured that people that we have punished for drug use can never rehabilitate themselves.

The other problem is the enormous corruption. We invaded Panama because President Bush called General Manuel Noriega an "international thug." As soon as the troops had secured the city a Drug Enforcement agent put handcuffs on General Noriega, who is now residing in a federal prison for 40 years. A year later that same DEA agent was himself arrested for stealing $720,000 in laundered drug money. The corruption has reached into our federal law enforcement; all throughout our nation we see the police corrupted, and the legal system paralyzed. Another heavy penalty we pay for the hysteria about these substances is that we have authorized seizure of private property. Remember that under criminal law if you are accused by the police of a crime, you are presumed innocent until you are proven guilty in court.

STATE AND FEDERAL PRISON POPULATION 1966–1996

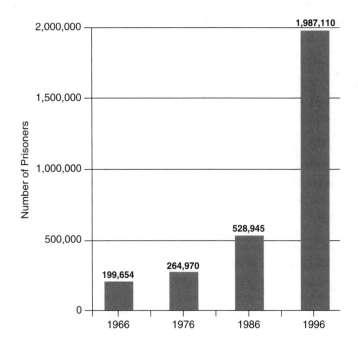

Source: U.S. Department of Justice, Bureau of Judicial Statistics, 1997.

Not so with seizure. Law enforcement authorities can seize a property if they suspect that it is used in a criminal enterprise, and you have to go to court to prove that you are innocent. They have seized more than $4 billion, without criminal conviction occurring in most cases. With the mere presence of suspicion, large amounts of cash, an "Informant" who said that you were involved with drugs, etc., they can take your house, your business, your car, and they have done this over and over again.

Drug education is another thing that the government talks about. The government has spent unprecedented amounts of money trying to educate young children not to use drugs. The DARE program (Drug Abuse Resistance Education) runs about $1 billion a year. It is taught by uniformed police officers in schools throughout the country, often financed by federal grants. Two studies commissioned by the government showed that DARE was ineffective. The government did not print or publish this study, which created an uproar in the research community. DARE had a constituency, and the government didn't want to lose that constituency by admitting that DARE had failed.

THE WAR IS OVER

We should declare the war is over. The mere word itself gives a connotation that anything goes, that all kinds of violations of search and seizure laws, all kinds of misconduct make sense, that the police can do anything because we are waging war against evil substances. We could immediately treat marijuana as we treat alcohol and cigarettes. There has never been a recorded death by marijuana, there has never been a recorded homicide caused by smoking pot. Prominent politicians and leaders Bill Clinton and Newt Gingrich have talked about how they experimented with pot. Now brain damage aside, neither of them went on to heroin or to commit armed bank robberies as far as we know.

We need to step back. Prohibition ended when President Hoover appointed a commission to study how Americans could be more law-abiding. The commission repealed Prohibition a few years later. Anyone who looks objectively at America's drug war will see that it is racist, violent, corrupt and unsuccessful.

"Drug prevention, education and treatment must be complemented by supply reduction abroad, interdiction on the borders and strong law enforcement within the United States."

THE WAR ON DRUGS CAN SUCCEED

Barry R. McCaffrey

Barry R. McCaffrey is director of the Office of National Drug Control Policy, the office commonly referred to as "drug czar." In the following viewpoint, McCaffrey maintains that the United States has made significant progress in reducing drug abuse since the 1970s. The fight against drug abuse, he says, can be won by implementing a multifaceted, long-term approach that includes treatment and prevention in addition to law enforcement and interdiction.

As you read, consider the following questions:

1. By how much has casual cocaine use dropped since 1985, according to the author?
2. What does McCaffrey say is the signature program of the government's ten-year approach?
3. How many Americans are in immediate need of drug treatment, according to the author?

Reprinted from Barry R. McCaffrey, "Confronting America's Drug Problem," *San Diego Union-Tribune*, August 2, 1998.

Americans should understand how successful our national anti-drug efforts have been. We have made enormous progress in our efforts to confront the cancer of drug abuse over the past two decades.

PROGRESS IN THE FIGHT AGAINST DRUG ABUSE

Casual drug use has dropped by 50 percent since 1979. Casual cocaine use has plummeted by 75 percent since 1985. Sixty-one million Americans who once used illegal drugs have rejected them. Eighty-five percent of Americans oppose legalization of cocaine, heroin and marijuana.

Drug-use rates have remained essentially stable since 1990. Just 6 percent of our population uses illegal drugs today. Unfortunately, some 4 million are chronically addicted and their number has not declined.

A MULTIFACETED APPROACH

The drug problem is multifaceted. As such, it requires a systemic, comprehensive solution. Our strategy includes prevention and treatment along with interdiction and law enforcement. We cannot succeed without all the component parts. We can make headway against this difficult problem by adopting a long-range approach that demands patience and perseverance. For this reason, the 1998 National Drug Control Strategy proposes a 10-year outlook supported by annually updated five-year budgets.

Our strategy aims to reduce drug-use rates by 50 percent in the coming decade. This will result in the lowest levels of use recorded in the past 30 years. Our strategy defines reduction in demand as the main focus of drug-control efforts. Prevention of drug, alcohol and tobacco use among our 68 million children and adolescents is our most important goal.

The strategy also recognizes that no single approach can solve the drug-abuse problem. Rather, drug prevention, education and treatment must be complemented by supply reduction abroad, interdiction on the borders and strong law enforcement within the United States.

The strategy ties public policy to a scientific, research-based body of knowledge. Our approach is also supported by a performance measurement system that includes short-, medium- and long-term targets for each of our five strategic goals. The measurement system allows for periodic review of successful initiatives and adjustments to the strategy as conditions change.

The signature program of this 10-year plan is the unprecedented five-year, $1 billion national anti-drug media campaign which President Bill Clinton and Speaker Newt Gingrich launched in Atlanta on July 9, 1998. Such an initiative is necessary because even though overall drug use in our country has dropped by half in the last 15 years, teen-age drug use has risen precipitously in the '90s. Eighth-grade use, for example, nearly tripled from 1992 to 1998.

Because mass media acts like a "proxy-peer" to our youth, defining the culture by identifying what's "cool" and what's not, a broad-based anti-drug campaign can counteract pro-drug messages that youngsters receive from many sources. Ad experts suggest that a minimum of four exposures a week which reach 90 percent of the target audience (mostly children but also parents, coaches, youth leaders and other adults who work with young people) will change attitudes and, in turn, behavior.

We have begun to shift federal spending priorities and programs in support of the five goals of the national strategy (which can be viewed on the World Wide Web at www.whitehousedrugpolicy.gov). Resources for prevention have increased 33 percent since 1996 while spending for treatment has increased by the same ratio since 1993. The Fiscal Year 1999 budget submitted by the president to Congress proposes spending an additional $506 million on prevention and treatment.

AN INAPPROPRIATE METAPHOR

Let us ask whether medicine is winning the war against death. The answer is obviously no, it isn't winning: the one fundamental rule of human existence remains, unfortunately, one man one death. And this is despite the fact that 14 percent of the gross domestic product of the United States (to say nothing of the efforts of other countries) goes into the fight against death. Was ever a war more expensively lost? Let us then abolish medical schools, hospitals, and departments of public health. If every man has to die, it doesn't matter very much when he does so.

If the war against drugs is lost, then so are the wars against theft, speeding, incest, fraud, rape, murder, arson, and illegal parking. Few, if any, such wars are winnable. So let us all do anything we choose.

Theodore Dalrymple, *City Journal*, Spring 1997.

Drug courts—which channel nonviolent drug-law offenders into tough, court-supervised treatment programs instead of prisons—represent our philosophy of dealing with drug users compassionately but firmly. The first drug court was established in Miami in 1989. In 1997, 20,000 defendants appeared before the nation's 215 drug courts, and 160 new ones are now in the planning stages.

Despite this record investment in demand reduction, drug treatment is available for only 52 percent of the 4 million Americans in immediate need and just 7 percent of addicted inmates. If drug use is to be reduced by half over the next 10 years, the nation's chronic users must be helped in overcoming drug dependence.

AN ONGOING EFFORT

The problem of drug abuse, like illness or warfare, will not go away in the foreseeable future. The so-called "war on drugs" is a poor metaphor because it creates the expectation of a speedy victory and a specific end to a campaign. We have suggested a metaphor of "cancer" as more appropriate for describing our strategy of prevention and treatment backed up by a high level of social and legal disapproval of drug use.

Like education, efforts against drug abuse must be ongoing in every generation. By way of example, we do not close schools, claiming we lost the "war on ignorance," because history, science and math must be taught year after year.

At the end of the day, we must all recognize that no single tactic—pursued alone or to the detriment of other possible and valuable initiatives—can work to contain or reduce the illegal drug problem that costs our society 14,000 dead and $110 billion a year. We will only make a dent in this problem if we have mutually supportive public-health and law-enforcement policies that are based on a strong dose of prevention.

| "The drug war is a futile, counterproductive, big-government program."

THE UNITED STATES SHOULD ABANDON THE WAR ON DRUGS

David Boaz

In the following viewpoint, David Boaz maintains that the war on drugs does far more harm than good. It has cost the country billions of dollars, he says, and caused increases in crime, corruption, and distrust of government. In the author's view, the drug war should be abandoned because it violates individual freedoms and because the majority of Americans do not support drug laws. David Boaz is vice president of the Cato Institute, a libertarian public policy research organization that advocates limited government.

As you read, consider the following questions:

1. What percentage of the prison population do drug offenders constitute, according to the author?
2. How does drug prohibition cause crime, in Boaz's view?
3. In the author's opinion, how does drug prohibition violate the Constitution?

On February 20, 1933, a new Congress acknowledged the failure of alcohol Prohibition and sent the Twenty-First Amendment to the states. Prohibition had begun in 1920 amid high hopes. Evangelist Billy Sunday proclaimed, "The reign of tears is over. The slums will soon be a memory. We will turn our prisons into factories and our jails into storehouses and corn-cribs. Men will walk upright now, women will smile and children will laugh. Hell will be forever for rent."

Alas, as historians of prohibitionist efforts could have predicted, Sunday was wrong. Congress recognized that Prohibition had failed to stop drinking and had increased prison populations and violent crime. By the end of 1933, national Prohibition was history, though many states continued to outlaw or severely restrict the sale of liquor.

THE FAILURE OF DRUG PROHIBITION

Today another Congress confronts a similarly failed prohibition policy. Futile efforts to enforce prohibition have been pursued even more vigorously in the 1980s and 1990s than they were in the 1920s. Total federal expenditures for the first 10 years of Prohibition amounted to $88 million—about $733 million in 1993 dollars. Drug enforcement cost about $22 billion in the Reagan years and another $45 billion in the four years of the Bush administration, and costs about $15 billion a year now.

Those mind-boggling amounts have had some effect. Total drug arrests are now more than 1 million a year. Since 1989, more people have been incarcerated for drug offenses than for all violent crimes combined, and drug offenders account for 60 percent of the federal prison population.

Yet as was the case during Prohibition, all the arrests and incarcerations haven't stopped the use and abuse of drugs, or the drug trade, or the crime associated with black-market transactions. Cocaine and heroin supplies are up; the more our Customs agents interdict, the more smugglers import.

There are at least a dozen reasons that today's prohibition should be repealed.

CRIME AND CORRUPTION

1) Drug prohibition causes crime. By driving up the price of drugs, prohibition forces drug users to commit crimes to pay for a habit that would be easily affordable if it were legal. And the outlaw nature of the business means that rival drug sellers must resort to violence to settle disputes among themselves. The per capita murder and assault-by-firearm rate rose steadily while

alcohol Prohibition was in effect (1920–33) and fell for 10 straight years after that. The murder rates generated by today's prohibition, of course, are much higher. Police officials have estimated that in many major cities as much as 50 percent of crime—including auto thefts, robberies and assaults, and burglaries—is committed by drug addicts to support their habits. It's not drug-related crime; it's prohibition-related crime. As conservatives say about guns, "If drugs are outlawed, only outlaws will sell drugs."

2) Drug prohibition corrupts law enforcement officials. The huge profits generated by prohibition are an irresistible temptation to Mexican drug czars, Colombian judges, American soldiers in Panama, police officers, agents of the Drug Enforcement Administration, and so on. When police officers and border guards arrest people carrying more cash than they'll make in a decade, it's hardly surprising that some of them are persuaded to look the other way.

3) Drug prohibition undermines respect for the law. When the government declares 25 million Americans criminals, and still can't enforce the drug laws, it chips away at the respect that underlies all law.

OTHER DAMAGE CAUSED BY DRUG PROHIBITION

4) Drug prohibition weakens the family. What kind of family structure can be maintained when a 13-year-old boy is paying his mother's rent out of his drug earnings? It is illegal drugs, not legal products, that are sold on school playgrounds and neighborhood streets.

5) Drug prohibition destroys the community. When the most successful people in an inner-city neighborhood are outlaws, the natural order of the community is inverted. The enormous profits generated by prohibition make a mockery of the work ethic and parental authority. Honesty, respect for private property, and all the other hallmarks of a civilized society are casualties of prohibition.

6) Drug prohibition reflects a failure to learn from history. We repealed the prohibition of alcohol because it produced crime, corruption, and social chaos. Now we are making the same mistakes and suffering the same consequences.

7) Drug prohibition is a classic example of throwing money at a problem. We spend $15 billion a year on enforcement of the drug laws—20 times as much in real terms as we ever spent on alcohol prohibition—to no avail. Drug prohibition is the sort of thing Ronald Reagan had in mind when he said, "The nearest

thing to eternal life on this earth is a government program."
President Bill Clinton's drug czar has now formally announced
that the War on Drugs will be endless.

Drug Prohibition Gives the Government Too Much Power

8) Drug prohibition centralizes power in Washington. The federal government has usurped the power of states and communities to determine their own policies, and the prosecution of the
drug war has caused federal law enforcement agencies to grow
at the expense of state and local police. Most recently, the Clinton administration refuses to accept the decision of the people
of Arizona and California to allow the medical use of marijuana,
and is threatening to arrest doctors who abide by state law. The
U.S. government has always seized on wars and emergencies to
expand its own powers at the expense of states, individuals, and
the Constitution.

Reprinted by permission of Chuck Asay and Creators Syndicate.

9) Drug prohibition does violence to civil liberties. There was
a time in this country when the government was only allowed
to punish someone after he was convicted in a court of law. It
now appears that the drug authorities can punish an American
citizen by seizing his car or his boat, not even after an indict-
ment—much less a conviction—but after a mere allegation by a

police officer. Whatever happened to the presumption of innocence? The demand to win this unwinnable war has led to wiretapping, entrapment, property seizures, and other abuses of Americans' traditional liberties.

10) Drug prohibition hurts our relations with our allies. When we pressure friendly Latin American governments to destroy their coca fields, we turn their citizens against them—and often into the arms of such leftist revolutionaries as Peru's Tupac Amaru—as well as stirring up their resentment of Yankee imperialism.

Drug Prohibition Is Unlawful

11) Drug prohibition does violence to the Constitution. The Tenth Amendment reserves to the states or the people all powers not granted to the federal government. At least the advocates of alcohol Prohibition had enough respect for the Constitution to seek a constitutional amendment to impose Prohibition, but Congress never asked the American people for the constitutional power to impose drug prohibition.

12) Drug prohibition violates individual rights. People have rights that governments may not violate. Thomas Jefferson defined them as the rights of life, liberty, and the pursuit of happiness. I would say that people have the right to live their lives in any way they choose so long as they don't violate the equal rights of others. What right could be more basic, more inherent in human nature, than the right to choose what substances to put in one's own body? Whether we're talking about alcohol, tobacco, AZT, saturated fat, medical marijuana, or recreational cocaine, this is a decision that should be made by the adult individual, not the government. If government can tell us what we can put into our own bodies, what can it not tell us? What limits on government action are there?

As William F. Buckley, Jr., says, "It is the duty of conservatives to declaim against lost causes when the ancillary results of pursuing them are tens of thousands of innocent victims and a gradual corruption of the machinery of the state." He's not the only leading conservative who recognizes the futility of the drug war. Sociologist Ernest van den Haag, Hoover Institution scholar Thomas Sowell, former secretary of state George Shultz, and Nobel laureate Milton Friedman agree with Buckley.

The drug war is a futile, counterproductive, big-government program. It is time to return the effort to control drug abuse to families, churches, schools, mission houses, and the other elements of civil society.

> "*We have a responsibility and an obligation . . . to protect our children, who are the primary victims of drug use.*"

THE UNITED STATES SHOULD CONTINUE THE WAR ON DRUGS

Charles E. Grassley

In the following viewpoint, Republican senator Charles E. Grassley argues that although the war on drugs is expensive, the United States has a responsibility to reduce the drug problem. Treatment, prevention, law enforcement, and interdiction are all vital parts of America's fight against drugs, he says. Some people have questioned the wisdom of U.S. drug policy, he contends, but such critics underestimate the severity of the drug problem and the ingenuity of drug dealers.

As you read, consider the following questions:
1. What is a conservative estimate of the cost of the U.S. anti-drug effort, according to Grassley?
2. What is responsible for the reduction in drug use among young people during the 1980s, according to the author?
3. How did drug dealer Carlos Lehder create demand for cocaine in the United States, according to the author?

Excerpted from Charles E. Grassley, "The U.S. Effort to Fight Drug Use," *Global Issues*, June 1997, www.usia.gov/journals/itgic/0697/ijge/gj-3.htm.

In 1997, the United States, at the federal level alone, allocated over $15,000 million. In the last 10 years, the United States has spent, again only at the federal level, $110,000 million to fight drugs. In addition to these sums, state and local governments in the United States have spent a comparable amount. On top of this, one must also include out-of-pocket efforts by businesses, communities, schools, and private individuals to deal with the range of problems associated with drug use. The conservative total from all these efforts adds up to close to $500,000 million. This figure does not count the indirect costs of drug use measured in human suffering, increased violence, and lost lives. What these numbers indicate is the terrible price the United States pays for its drug problem. It also indicates an abiding willingness on the part of the government and the people to fight back.

The government and the American public are committed to this effort for one simple reason: kids. It is an unfortunate fact that the most vulnerable population for drug use—whether in the United States or in other countries—is children. The original drug epidemic in the United States occurred among teenagers and young adults, many as young as 15 and 16. Today, the target for drug pushers are kids as young as 11 and 12. No country can sit by passively and watch as its future is consumed by a plague that destroys lives and creates problems for future generations. No responsible government can passively accept such a situation. That is why the United States devotes resources, time, and effort to the war on drugs, at home and abroad.

U.S. DRUG CONTROL STRATEGY

The U.S. effort at home consumes the overwhelming majority of federal funds and, of course, all the monies spent by state, local, and private groups. This totals more than $30,000 million annually. Federal counter-drug resources are spent in four main areas: treatment, prevention, law enforcement, and international programs. Considerable sums are also allocated to research in these same areas. The totals, in thousands of millions of dollars for 1997 and 1998, are as follows:

Drug Function	FY97	FY98
Law Enforcement	$7,835	$8,126
Treatment	$2,808	>$3,003
Prevention	$1,648	$1,916
International	$450	$487
Interdiction	$1,638	$1,609
Research and Intelligence	$723	$831

In 1988, Congress created the Office of National Drug Control Policy, the "Drug Czar", to coordinate all federal drug control programs. Congress requires the administration to present each year a national drug control strategy. As part of that strategy, the law requires the administration to submit a consolidated budget based on the strategy. . . . This budget represents a national commitment to deal with the drug problem in all its aspects.

Law enforcement resources in the budget cover a number of activities, including investigations, court proceedings, incarceration costs, and small sums for drug treatment programs in prisons. This request also includes some $10 million, for example, to the National Forest Service to combat illegal marijuana production in several parks. It includes support to state governments for marijuana crop eradication.

TREATMENT AND PREVENTION

Treatment assistance goes to support treatment programs for addicts across the country. The majority of these funds are provided in bloc grants to states to administer. This money supports a variety of treatment efforts, from long-term residential programs to various forms of intervention programs designed to help addicts. Unfortunately, there is no cure for drug addiction and treatment is often a lifelong undertaking. This is why we also support prevention efforts. The goal is to persuade potential users to never start. The majority of the prevention funds are allocated to individual states to promote education in schools and to support community coalition efforts to keep kids off drugs. In addition to these efforts, I am also working in Congress to pass legislation that would provide resources to communities for drug prevention.

It is our experience that when parents, community leaders, schools, businesses, religious leaders, and students commit to drug prevention, we see the best results. Community efforts in Miami and in Cincinnati today serve as clear models and success stories. Our experiences during the 1980s and early 1990s also serve as an example. During those years, major efforts among the nation's young people dramatically reduced experimentation with drugs. Teenage drug use dropped by more than 50 percent, cocaine use by more than 70 percent between 1980 and 1990. Moreover, attitudes about the dangers of drug use similarly changed, the growing perception among young people being that drugs were dangerous and wrong. We achieved these declines despite the fact that drugs remained available.

International Efforts

In addition to the resources that the United States devotes to control the domestic problems of drug use, we also spend considerable sums to interdict drugs at and beyond our borders. We support international efforts to stop the illegal production and transit of drugs overseas. Virtually all the drugs consumed in the United States are produced illegally in Asia and Latin America and smuggled into this country by major criminal organizations based outside the United States. Since 1992, the United States has spent over $500 million in Colombia, Bolivia, and Peru alone to support law enforcement, interdiction, alternative development, treatment and prevention, and military support. This money has gone to assist in local efforts to combat not only illegal drug production but also to deal with the threats posed by major criminal organizations that use violence, intimidation, and corruption to undermine the integrity of the courts, businesses, and political leaders.

Reducing the Drug Supply Is Critical

In the two years since Peruvian President Alberto Fujimori implemented a get-tough, antitrafficking and crop-eradication program—including shooting down drug smugglers' aircraft—cocaine production in Peru has dropped 40 percent. With more U.S. support, victory over the narcotics trade in Peru is within reach. The same could be accomplished in Bolivia and Colombia with the cooperation of their governments and a continued U.S. effort to keep radar and tracking planes in the air 24 hours a day.

A continued investment in demand-reduction strategies is critical. I strongly support finding ways to persuade Americans that doing drugs is wrong—that it destroys lives, families, schools and communities. But we need a comprehensive counter-drug strategy that addresses all components of this problem. The lesson of the past decade is simple: Prevent drugs from entering the country and you drive up the price of drugs. Drive up the price of drugs and you save lives.

Bill McCollum, *Insight*, September 14, 1998.

U.S. efforts to combat drugs have not stopped at spending money on the problem. The United States, particularly the Congress, has pioneered legislation to create the appropriate legal framework to combat drug production and money laundering. In this regard, the United States created some of the first major anti–money laundering and criminal enterprise legislation.

These include reporting requirements on bank deposits on sums over $10,000 as a means to prevent large cash and non-cash transactions to disguise the sources of the money. These laws also include confiscation provisions that permit the seizure of assets directly and indirectly acquired as a result of drug smuggling and selling. These laws have been aggressively employed against individuals involved in the drug trade, in the United States and abroad.

As part of the effort to control drug production, the United States also pioneered legislation to control the sale and transit of the precursor chemicals used in the production of illegal drugs. This law gave U.S. law enforcement agencies a powerful tool to prevent the diversion of key chemical components in drug production. The United States has encouraged other countries to adopt similar laws and has worked with individual companies to develop self-regulating mechanisms. Unfortunately, many countries have yet to adopt rigorous standards to actively enforce existing laws.

As part of its overall efforts to promote comprehensive drug control, the United States has also worked with the international community. The United States has worked with the G-7 countries [the Group of Seven industrialized nations] to promote international standards for appropriate financial controls through the Financial Action Task Force. Congress has also put great emphasis on international compliance with the 1988 U.N. Convention on Psychotropic Drugs. In addition, the United States has supplied money to the United Nations Drug Control Program to promote treatment prevention, crop eradication, and alternative development projects in many different countries. All of these efforts, along with domestic programs, are part of on-going progress to deal with the range of problems created by international drug production, trafficking, and use.

BOTH SUPPLY AND DEMAND MUST BE REDUCED

There are a variety of misconceptions about the drug problem in general and what the United States is doing about it. The biggest misconception involves oversimplified distinctions made between supply and demand. The most common argument is that if Americans did not consume drugs—no demand—there would be no incentive to produce and smuggle drugs—no supply. While this seems plausible, it does not reflect the complexity of the relationship between supply and demand generally or with drugs more specifically.

In many cases, it is supply that drives or creates demand. No new product, for example, for which there is no current market, begins with demand. The creator and manufacturer of the product must create the demand through marketing, pricing, and advertising. Similarly, when a business wants to break into a market, it will often try to flood the market with large quantities of its goods at low prices. This is true whether we are talking about computer chips or cocaine. The criminal organizations involved in drug production are big businesses and many of their practices and activities mirror those of legitimate business. Like many legal enterprises before them, they recognized that the United States was the world's largest market. For drug traffickers, breaking into the American market was tapping into the opportunity for huge profits. As part of a business strategy, these groups targeted the American market and aggressively worked to create a demand for their product.

DEALERS CREATED DEMAND FOR COCAINE

The evolution of these activities is easy to trace. The United States in the early 1970s had no serious cocaine problem. Use was confined to the cultural elite with the money to pay the high price for the drugs. Carlos Lehder, an enterprising smuggler, realized the possibilities for creating a new market. Using his connections in Colombia and his smuggling networks, he began to increase the supply of cocaine in the United States. He targeted middle class users. By dramatically increasing the supply and lowering the price, he made cocaine more available, helping to create a demand. Once the demand began to grow, supply and demand began to complement one another. While he was doing this, U.S. law enforcement and policy makers missed the significance of what was happening. It was not until there was an explosion of violence and spreading addiction problems that authorities realized what was going on. By then, cocaine had established itself across the country as a major drug of choice.

A similar story can be told about the rapid expansion of methamphetamine use in the United States. The drug organizations are also expanding their user networks in Latin America, the Caribbean, and Mexico. They are paying local traffickers in drugs. They are offering drugs at very low costs or, in some cases, giving it away, in order to build a base of users. Unfortunately, one of the characteristics of drug supply and demand is that large supplies at affordable prices drives demand. No country is immune to this pattern.

In discussing this aspect of the drug problem, I am not arguing that the United States has no responsibility to deal with drug use. Quite the contrary. We have a responsibility and an obligation, not only as responsible members of the international community but also as parents trying to protect our children, who are the primary victims of drug use. My point in discussing the issue of supply and demand is to make clear that the problem is not a simple one. There is a further issue to consider in addressing this misconception. It is a moral question. The question is simply put: Who is more responsible for the drug problem, the person who chooses to use illegal drugs, or the person who produces, transits, and sells them? There are no simple answers, but the point is that neither producing countries nor consumers can afford to ignore the problems created by illegal drugs. Serious efforts to fight back are not the result of simplistic distinctions between supply and demand, especially if they are an attempt to shift responsibility in order to do nothing. . . .

[Another] misconception that percolates through the debate on drugs is that the United States does nothing to deal with its own problem. I hope that my earlier remarks address that misconception.

There is one further issue in this vein that I wish to address, and that is the notion that legalizing drug use would solve all the problems. In this view, simply legalizing dangerous drugs for personal use would end criminal activities, would reduce the harm of punitive legal steps against consenting users, and would do away with the need for the whole, expensive architecture of enforcement. None of these views is accurate. Indeed, as a formula for public policy they court disaster. At a minimum, they would dramatically increase the number of current users of dangerous drugs. Rather than reduce the harm currently caused by drugs, they would redistribute the harm to a large number of individuals and foist the costs for this onto the public purse.

There is no royal road to a solution of our drug problem, either supply or demand. What is required is determination to deal with the problem, a willingness to act, and stamina to stay the course. The consequences of failure mean losing more kids and giving free reign to the criminal thugs that push the drugs.

"Drugs are here to stay, and . . . we
have no choice but to learn how to
live with them so that they cause
the least possible harm."

U.S. DRUG POLICY SHOULD INCORPORATE PRINCIPLES OF HARM REDUCTION

Ethan A. Nadelmann

Ethan A. Nadelmann argues in the following viewpoint that U.S.
drug policy has failed because of its unrealistic goal of completely eradicating drug use. A more effective policy, he says,
would acknowledge that some drug abuse is inevitable and con-
centrate on minimizing the damage associated with drug abuse.
The author maintains that America can benefit by following the
examples of several European countries that have successfully
implemented harm reduction policies, including needle exchange programs to reduce the spread of AIDS and methadone
treatment for heroin addicts. Nadelmann is director of the Lindesmith Center, a drug-policy research institute in New York City.

As you read, consider the following questions:

1. How many cases of HIV infection could have been avoided if
   the United States had adopted needle exchange programs,
   according to the author?
2. What is the view of the National Academy of Sciences
   regarding methadone maintenance, as quoted by
   Nadelmann?
3. How do rates of marijuana and cocaine use in the
   Netherlands compare with those in the Unites States,
   according to the author?

Excerpted from Ethan A. Nadelmann, "Commonsense Drug Policy," *Foreign Affairs*,
January/February 1998. Reprinted by permission of *Foreign Affairs*. Copyright 1998 by the
Council on Foreign Relations, Inc.

In 1988 Congress passed a resolution proclaiming its goal of "a drug-free America by 1995." U.S. drug policy has failed persistently over the decades because it has preferred such rhetoric to reality, and moralism to pragmatism. Politicians confess their youthful indiscretions, then call for tougher drug laws. Drug control officials make assertions with no basis in fact or science. Police officers, generals, politicians, and guardians of public morals qualify as drug czars—but not, to date, a single doctor or public health figure. Independent commissions are appointed to evaluate drug policies, only to see their recommendations ignored as politically risky. And drug policies are designed, implemented, and enforced with virtually no input from the millions of Americans they affect most: drug users. Drug abuse is a serious problem, both for individual citizens and society at large, but the "war on drugs" has made matters worse, not better. . . .

Imagine instead a policy that starts by acknowledging that drugs are here to stay, and that we have no choice but to learn how to live with them so that they cause the least possible harm. Imagine a policy that focuses on reducing not illicit drug use per se but the crime and misery caused by both drug abuse and prohibitionist policies. And imagine a drug policy based not on the fear, prejudice, and ignorance that drive America's current approach but rather on common sense, science, public health concerns, and human rights. Such a policy is possible in the United States, especially if Americans are willing to learn from the experiences of other countries where such policies are emerging. . . .

ATTITUDES ABROAD

The harm-reduction approaches spreading throughout Europe and Australia and even into corners of North America show promise. These approaches start by acknowledging that supply-reduction initiatives are inherently limited, that criminal justice responses can be costly and counterproductive, and that single-minded pursuit of a "drug-free society" is dangerously quixotic. Demand-reduction efforts to prevent drug abuse among children and adults are important, but so are harm-reduction efforts to lessen the damage to those unable or unwilling to stop using drugs immediately, and to those around them.

Most proponents of harm reduction do not favor legalization. They recognize that prohibition has failed to curtail drug abuse, that it is responsible for much of the crime, corruption, disease, and death associated with drugs, and that its costs mount every year. But they also see legalization as politically unwise and as risking increased drug use. The challenge is thus making drug prohibition work better, but with a focus on reducing the negative consequences of both drug use and prohibitionist policies.

Countries that have turned to harm-reduction strategies for help in alleviating their drug woes are not so different from the United States. Drugs, crime, and race problems, and other socioeconomic problems are inextricably linked. As in America, criminal justice authorities still prosecute and imprison major drug traffickers as well as petty dealers who create public nuisances. Parents worry that their children might get involved with drugs. Politicians remain fond of drug war rhetoric. But by contrast with U.S. drug policy, public health goals have priority, and public health authorities have substantial influence. Doctors have far more latitude in treating addiction and associated problems. Police view the sale and use of illicit drugs as similar to prostitution—vice activities that cannot be stamped out but can be effectively regulated. Moralists focus less on any inherent evils of drugs than on the need to deal with drug use and addiction pragmatically and humanely. And more politicians dare to speak out in favor of alternatives to punitive prohibitionist policies. . . .

Stopping HIV with Sterile Syringes

The spread of HIV, the virus that causes AIDS, among people who inject drugs illegally was what prompted governments in Europe and Australia to experiment with harm-reduction policies. During the early 1980s public health officials realized that infected users were spreading HIV by sharing needles. Having already experienced a hepatitis epidemic attributed to the same mode of transmission, the Dutch were the first to tell drug users about the risks of needle sharing and to make sterile syringes available and collect dirty needles through pharmacies, needle exchange and methadone programs, and public health services. Governments elsewhere in Europe and in Australia soon followed suit. The few countries in which a prescription was necessary to obtain a syringe dropped the requirement. Local authorities in Germany, Switzerland, and other European countries authorized needle exchange machines to ensure 24-hour access. In some European cities, addicts can exchange used syringes for clean ones at local police stations without fear of prosecution or harassment. Prisons are instituting similar policies to help discourage the spread of HIV among inmates, recognizing that illegal drug injecting cannot be eliminated even behind bars.

These initiatives were not adopted without controversy. Conservative politicians argued that needle exchange programs condoned illicit and immoral behavior and that government policies should focus on punishing drug users or making them drug-free. But by the late 1980s, the consensus in most of Western Europe, Oceania, and Canada was that while drug abuse was a serious problem, AIDS was worse. Slowing the spread of a fatal disease for which no cure exists was the greater moral imperative. There was also a fiscal imperative. Needle exchange programs' costs are minuscule compared with those of treating people who would otherwise become infected with HIV.

IRRATIONAL U.S. POLICY

Only in the United States has this logic not prevailed, even though AIDS was the leading killer of Americans ages 25 to 44 for most of the 1990s and is now No. 2. The Centers for Disease Control (CDC) estimates that half of new HIV infections in the country stem from injection drug use. Yet both the White House and Congress block allocation of AIDS or drug-abuse prevention funds for needle exchange. . . .

Governments at all levels in the United States refuse to fund needle exchange for political reasons, even though dozens of scientific studies, domestic and foreign, have found that needle exchange and other distribution programs reduce needle sharing, bring hard-to-reach drug users into contact with health care systems, and inform addicts about treatment programs, yet do not increase illegal drug use. . . .

To date, America's failure in this regard is conservatively estimated to have resulted in the infection of up to 10,000 people with HIV. Mounting scientific evidence and the stark reality of the continuing AIDS crisis have convinced the public, if not politicians, that needle exchange saves lives; polls consistently find that a majority of Americans support needle exchange, with approval highest among those most familiar with the notion. Prejudice and political cowardice are poor excuses for allowing more citizens to suffer from and die of AIDS, especially when effective interventions are cheap, safe, and easy.

METHADONE AND OTHER ALTERNATIVES

The United States pioneered the use of the synthetic opiate methadone to treat heroin addiction in the 1960s and 1970s, but now lags behind much of Europe and Australia in making methadone accessible and effective. Methadone is the best available treatment in terms of reducing illicit heroin use and associated crime, disease, and death. In the early 1990s the National

Academy of Sciences' Institute of Medicine stated that of all forms of drug treatment, "methadone maintenance has been the most rigorously studied modality and has yielded the most incontrovertibly positive results. . . . Consumption of all illicit drugs, especially heroin, declines. Crime is reduced, fewer individuals become HIV positive, and individual functioning is improved." However, the institute went on to declare, "Current policy . . . puts too much emphasis on protecting society from methadone, and not enough on protecting society from the epidemics of addiction, violence, and infectious diseases that methadone can help reduce."

CANNABIS, COCAINE, AND HEROIN USE AMONG STUDENTS IN SECONDARY SCHOOLS (AGES 13 TO 18 YEARS) IN THE NETHERLANDS AND THE USA

Lifetime	13–14 Years		15–16 Years		17–18 Years	
	USA	NL	USA	NL	USA	NL
Cannabis	14.6%	2.6%	35.0%	10.8%	43.7%	17.7%
Cocaine	3.6%	.6%	7.7%	1.2%	10.3%	1.6%
Heroin	NA		1.3%	0.5%		

Month	13–14 Years		15–16 Years		17–18 Years	
	USA	NL	USA	NL	USA	NL
Cannabis	5.4%	1.3%	14.9%	5.2%	16.7%	4.6%
Cocaine	1.6%	1.2%	2.7%	0.5%	2.8%	0.2%
Heroin	NA		0.3%	0.3%		

Source: Michael Elsner, *The Sociology of Reefer Madness: The Criminalization of Marijuana in the USA* (Washington, D.C.: Unpublished Ph.D. Dissertation, American University, 1994).

Methadone is to street heroin what nicotine skin patches and chewing gum are to cigarettes—with the added benefit of legality. Taken orally, methadone has little of injected heroin's effect on mood or cognition. It can be consumed for decades with few if any negative health consequences, and its purity and concentration, unlike street heroin's, are assured. Like other opiates, it can create physical dependence if taken regularly, but the "addiction" is more like a diabetic's "addiction" to insulin than a heroin addict's to product bought on the street. Methadone patients can and do drive safely, hold good jobs, and care for their children. When prescribed adequate doses, they can be indistinguishable from people who have never used heroin or methadone.

CONDEMNING AN EFFECTIVE TREATMENT

Popular misconceptions and prejudice, however, have all but prevented any expansion of methadone treatment in the United States. The 115,000 Americans receiving methadone today represent only a small increase over the number 20 years ago. For every ten heroin addicts, there are only one or two methadone treatment slots. Methadone is the most tightly controlled drug in the pharmacopoeia, subject to unique federal and state restrictions. Doctors cannot prescribe it for addiction treatment outside designated programs. Regulations dictate not only security, documentation, and staffing requirements but maximum doses, admission criteria, time spent in the program, and a host of other specifics, none of which has much to do with quality of treatment. Moreover, the regulations do not prevent poor treatment; many clinics provide insufficient doses, prematurely detoxify clients, expel clients for offensive behavior, and engage in other practices that would be regarded as unethical in any other field of medicine. Attempts to open new clinics tend to be blocked by residents who don't want addicts in their neighborhood. . . .

EUROPEAN EXPERIMENTS WITH HEROIN MAINTENANCE

In England, doctors have broad discretion to prescribe whatever drugs help addicted patients manage their lives and stay away from illegal drugs and their dealers. Beginning in the 1920s, thousands of English addicts were maintained on legal prescriptions of heroin, morphine, amphetamine, cocaine, and other pharmaceutical drugs. This tradition flourished until the 1960s, and has reemerged in response to AIDS and to growing disappointment with the Americanization of British prescribing practices during the 1970s and 1980s, when illicit heroin use in Britain increased almost tenfold. Doctors in other European countries and Australia are also trying heroin prescription.

The Swiss government began a nationwide trial in 1994 to determine whether prescribing heroin, morphine, or injectable methadone could reduce crime, disease, and other drug-related ills. Some 1,000 volunteers—only heroin addicts with at least two unsuccessful experiences in methadone or other conventional treatment programs were considered—took part in the experiment. The trial quickly determined that virtually all participants preferred heroin, and doctors subsequently prescribed it for them. In 1997 the government reported the results so far: criminal offenses and the number of criminal offenders dropped 60 percent, the percentage of income from illegal and semilegal activities fell from 69 to 10 percent, illegal heroin and cocaine use declined dramatically (although use of alcohol, cannabis, and tranquilizers like Valium remained fairly constant), stable employment increased from 14 to 32 percent, physical health improved enormously, and most participants greatly reduced their contact with the drug scene. There were no deaths from overdoses, and no prescribed drugs were diverted to the black market. More than half those who dropped out of the study switched to another form of drug treatment, including 83 who began abstinence therapy. A cost-benefit analysis of the program found a net economic benefit of $30 per patient per day, mostly because of reduced criminal justice and health care costs.

LESSONS OF THE SWISS EXPERIENCE

The Swiss study has undermined several myths about heroin and its habitual users. The results to date demonstrate that, given relatively unlimited availability, heroin users will voluntarily stabilize or reduce their dosage and some will even choose abstinence; that long-addicted users can lead relatively normal, stable lives if provided legal access to their drug of choice; and that ordinary citizens will support such initiatives. In recent referendums in Zurich, Basel, and Zug, substantial majorities voted to continue funding local arms of the experiment. In 1997, a nationwide referendum to end the government's heroin maintenance and other harm-reduction initiatives was rejected by 71 percent of Swiss voters, including majorities in all 26 cantons. . . .

Switzerland, attempting to reduce overdoses, dangerous injecting practices, and shooting up in public places, has also taken the lead in establishing "safe injection rooms" where users can inject their drugs under secure, sanitary conditions. There are now about a dozen such rooms in the country, and initial evaluations are positive. In Germany, Frankfurt has set up three, and there are also officially sanctioned facilities in Hamburg and Saarbrücken. Cities elsewhere in Europe and in Australia are expected to open safe injection rooms soon.

REEFER SANITY

Cannabis, in the form of marijuana and hashish, is by far the most popular illicit drug in the United States. More than a quarter of Americans admit to having tried it. Marijuana's popularity peaked in 1980, dropped steadily until the early 1990s, and is now on the rise again. Although it is not entirely safe, especially when consumed by children, smoked heavily, or used when driving, it is clearly among the least dangerous psychoactive drugs in common use. In 1988 the administrative law judge for the Drug Enforcement Administration, Francis Young, reviewed the evidence and concluded that "marihuana, in its natural form, is one of the safest therapeutically active substances known to man."

As with needle exchange and methadone treatment, American politicians have ignored or spurned the findings of government commissions and scientific organizations concerning marijuana policy. In 1972 the National Commission on Marihuana and Drug Abuse—created by President Richard Nixon and chaired by a former Republican governor, Raymond Shafer—recommended that possession of up to one ounce of marijuana be decriminalized. Nixon rejected the recommendation. In 1982 a panel appointed by the National Academy of Sciences reached the same conclusion as the Shafer Commission. . . .

MARIJUANA CRIMINALIZATION HAS BEEN INEFFECTIVE

Between 1973 and 1989, annual arrests on marijuana charges by state and local police ranged between 360,000 and 460,000. The annual total fell to 283,700 in 1991, but has since more than doubled. In 1996, 641, 642 people were arrested for marijuana, 85 percent of them for possession, not sale, of the drug. Prompted by concern over rising marijuana use among adolescents and fears of being labeled soft on drugs, the Clinton administration launched its own anti-marijuana campaign in 1995. But the administration's claims to have identified new risks of marijuana consumption—including a purported link between marijuana and violent behavior—have not withstood scrutiny. Neither Congress nor the White House seems likely to put the issue of marijuana policy before a truly independent advisory commission, given the consistency with which such commissions have reached politically unacceptable conclusions.

In contrast, governments in Europe and Australia, notably in the Netherlands, have reconsidered their cannabis policies. In 1976 the Baan Commission in the Netherlands recommended, and the Dutch government adopted, a policy of separating the "soft" and "hard" drug markets. Criminal penalties for and police efforts against heroin trafficking were increased, while those against cannabis were relaxed. Marijuana and hashish can now be bought in hundreds of "coffeeshops" throughout the country. Advertising, open displays, and sales to minors are prohibited. Police quickly close coffeeshops caught selling hard drugs. Almost no one is arrested or even fined for cannabis possession, and the government collects taxes on the gray market sales.

In the Netherlands today, cannabis consumption for most age

groups is similar to that in the United States. Young Dutch teen-agers, however, are less likely to sample marijuana than their American peers; from 1992 to 1994, only 7.2 percent of Dutch youths between the ages of 12 and 15 reported having tried marijuana, compared to 13.5 percent of Americans in that age bracket. Far fewer Dutch youths, moreover, experiment with co-caine, buttressing officials' claims of success in separating the markets for hard and soft drugs. Most Dutch parents regard the "reefer madness" anti-marijuana campaigns of the United States as silly. . . .

GROWING SUPPORT

Support for harm-reduction approaches is growing in the United States, notably and vocally among public health professionals but also, more discreetly, among urban politicians and police officials. Some of the world's most innovative needle exchange and other harm-reduction programs can be found in America. The 1996 victories at the polls for California's Proposition 215, which le-galizes the medicinal use of marijuana, and Arizona's Proposition 200, which allows doctors to prescribe any drug they deem ap-propriate and mandates treatment rather than jail for those ar-rested for possession, suggest that Americans are more receptive to drug policy reform than politicians acknowledge.

But Europe and Australia are generally ahead of the United States in their willingness to discuss openly and experiment pragmatically with alternative policies that might reduce the harm to both addicts and society. Public health officials in many European cities work closely with police, politicians, private physicians, and others to coordinate efforts. Community polic-ing treats drug dealers and users as elements of the community that need not be expelled but can be made less troublesome. Such efforts, including crackdowns on open drug scenes in Zurich, Bern, and Frankfurt, are devised and implemented in tandem with initiatives to address health and housing problems. In the United States, in contrast, politicians presented with new approaches do not ask, "Will they work?" but only, "Are they tough enough?" Many legislators are reluctant to support drug treatment programs that are not punitive, coercive, and prison-based, and many criminal justice officials still view prison as a quick and easy solution for drug problems.

The lessons from Europe and Australia are compelling. Drug control policies should focus on reducing drug-related crime, disease, and death, not the number of casual drug users. Stop-ping the spread of HIV by and among drug users by making sterile syringes and methadone readily available must be the first priority. American politicians need to explore, not ignore or automatically condemn, promising policy options such as cannabis decriminalization, heroin prescription, and the integration of harm-reduction principles into community policing strategies. Central governments must back, or at least not hinder, the efforts of municipal officials and citizens to devise pragmatic approaches to local drug problems. Like citizens in Europe, the American public has supported such innovations when they are adequately explained and allowed to prove themselves. As the evidence comes in, what works is increasingly apparent. All that remains is mustering the political courage.

"Harm reduction entails enabling [drug] users to continue their self-destructive behavior."

U.S. DRUG POLICY SHOULD NOT INCORPORATE PRINCIPLES OF HARM REDUCTION

Part I: Robert L. Maginnis, Part II: Sally Satel

In the following two-part viewpoint, psychiatrist Sally Satel and policy analyst Robert L. Maginnis argue that the philosophy of harm reduction is misguided. In Part I, Robert L. Maginnis maintains that harm reduction policies exacerbate the problem of drug abuse. He says that zero tolerance of drug abuse is a better approach, but he warns that harm reduction advocates are gaining influence in government. In Part II, Sally Satel discusses the meeting of the First International Conference on Heroin Maintenance in New York City on June 6, 1998. Heroin maintenance, she says, is a disastrous experiment in harm reduction, and its failure illustrates the faults of harm reduction. Maginnis is a senior policy analyst at the Family Research Council, an education and research organization in Washington, D.C.; Satel is a psychiatrist at the Yale University School of Medicine.

As you read, consider the following questions:

1. What is Ethan Nadelmann's opinion of drug legalization, as quoted by Maginnis?
2. According to Satel, what changes to its drug policy does the Swiss government plan to implement by 2004?
3. What does Satel say is the "raw truth about harm reduction"?

I

"Harm reduction" is a new approach to the drug abuse crisis which is winning disciples worldwide. Its goal is to legalize drugs, stop illicit substance interdiction efforts and step up abuse treatment.

The "harm reduction" approach maintains that drug abuse is inevitable and that society must learn to accept the "responsible use" of psychoactive substances. It ignores the physiological and psychological effects of illicit drugs, preferring concepts that include outright legalization of all drugs or non-enforcement of existing drug laws. There is evidence that the United States is embracing "harm reduction.". . .

HARM REDUCTION'S POPULARITY

- There are at least 75 needle giveaway programs in 55 American cities. These programs give needles to addicts to ostensibly slow the spread of the AIDS virus, but there is evidence that high-risk drug abusers are at least as likely to contract the disease through sexual contact. Moreover, giving needles encourages drug abuse. Some of these programs are paid for with tax dollars.
- Conservative columnist William F. Buckley Jr. has joined the harm reduction camp. The February 1996 edition of *National Review* featured Buckley and six "harm reduction" proponents agreeing that the drug war has failed and calling for decriminalization of illicit drugs.
- Billionaire philanthropist George Soros has given $15 million to fund organizations that actively promote harm reduction programs. Soros was also the major financial backer for California's 1996 medical marijuana ballot initiative and has financed many needle giveaway programs.
- Major television networks have featured news magazines that sympathetically portray harm reduction as an answer to the "failed" drug war. On April 6, 1995, ABC's Catherine Crier began her news magazine, "America's War on Drugs— Searching for Solutions" with the statement, "If America cannot win the war on drugs, it should try instead to reduce the harm associated with drug abuse."
- The Clinton administration has overseen a "controlled shift" in drug policy from an aggressive interdiction policy to one of harm reduction. The federal government's ability to disrupt drug shipments has been reduced by 64 percent. Foreign anti-drug programs have been cut by 55 percent and

domestic marijuana eradication by 59 percent. Meanwhile, between 1992 and 1996 funds for treatment rose 19 percent.

Harm reduction was appropriated from the safety and insurance industries. These industries try to minimize the consequences and probabilities of accidents and costly illnesses by providing incentives for behaviors like wearing safety belts, not smoking, exercising regularly and avoiding high-risk sports such as skydiving and auto racing. This business philosophy has been transferred into drug-related public policy.

The Netherlands was the first country to adopt a "harm reduction" public policy. In the 1970s, the Dutch responded to an outbreak of hepatitis among injection drug users by passing out clean needles. The concept gained momentum with the AIDS epidemic and quickly spread across Europe. Harm reducers have expanded the concept to include heroin maintenance programs, legalization of marijuana and reduced interdiction and enforcement efforts. . . .

ZERO TOLERANCE IS BETTER

The American Civil Liberties Union's AIDS project is a leading promoter of "harm reduction" in America. "Harm reduction attempts to instrumentalize the notion of meeting individuals 'where they're at,'" says the ACLU, "by providing each user with as many techniques and tools as possible to reduce that user's particular drug-related problems." It labels "harm reduction" the "safe sex" approach to preventing drug abuse.

The whole harm reduction approach is a complete reversal of the "zero tolerance" nature of this nation's recent drug policy. According to the ACLU, harm reduction "assumes that drug users' civil rights and individual autonomy should be respected, treats drug users as important participants in the process of gaining or maintaining control over their drug use, and makes no moral judgment based solely upon an individual's use of drugs."

Wayne Roques, a retired Drug Enforcement Administration agent, disagrees. "Harm reduction entails enabling the users to continue their self-destructive behavior," says Roques. "It is more logical to reduce the demand for drugs by improving and expanding law enforcement, education, prevention, research, rehabilitation and recovery programs.". . .

HARM REDUCTION OVERSEAS

Harm reduction advocates are quick to tout the successes of foreign drug policy experiments. They suggest that America should declare defeat and mimic foreign drug policy. On close examination, the foreign "experiments" may well represent yet another form of defeat.

The European Cities on Drug Policy (ECDP) is the primary torch-bearer for Europe's harm reduction philosophy. In 1990, the city of Frankfurt/Main, Germany hosted ECDP's first international conference which included officials from 22 cities and regions. That conference adopted the so-called Frankfurt Resolution which called for heroin distribution to drug addicts, decriminalization of cannabis and the introduction of shooting galleries (safe havens for abusers to inject illicit drugs). Today, it encourages other cities and nations to embrace the tenets of harm reduction. One of its first disciples was Scotland.

"Harm reduction really sounds good," says Kerry Condron, 18, a heroin addict from Glasgow, Scotland, "but it doesn't work." Condron says that harm reduction has become another way of perpetuating addiction.

Glasgow's harm reduction goal was to prevent the spread of AIDS and to reduce crime. Drug addicts were given clean needles and methadone, a heroin substitute.

Maxie Richards runs a home for Glasgow addicts. She says that harm reduction has become a vested interest of the social service industry, and with only one purpose: keeping social peace at the cost of dispensing drugs. She argues that social workers have too much power. According to Richards, the harm reduction approach says, "If you have to take drugs we can live with it." In fact, harm reduction policies are often harmful.

Richards' views on harm reduction needle-exchanges have scientific support. The August 3, 1996 edition of *The Lancet*, a respected British medical journal, profiled a Montreal, Canada study which found that injection drug users were two times more likely to become infected with HIV than those who did not. Researcher Julie Bruneau said that the increased HIV risks were "substantial and consistent . . . despite extensive adjustments for confounders."

NORMALIZING DRUG USE IN THE NETHERLANDS

The Dutch say they want to "normalize" addicts through their harm reduction policy. They do this by providing social services such as medical care, housing, free methadone and needles. About half of Amsterdam's [the largest Dutch city] 400 general medical practitioners prescribe methadone for their patients.

"Normalizing" includes providing clean needles to addicts. Ton Quadt, the Rotterdam coordinator of all drug treatment programs, says, "If you put in enough clean syringes and needles, people don't have to use dirty needles, so the risk of getting HIV is lessened, and I think the Dutch number will prove it."

Studies of the Dutch policy provide some revealing numbers indeed. In 1993, Dr. Karl Gunning, a Dutch physician and a harm reduction opponent, wrote, "The harm reduction Dutch policy of containing heroin addiction through distribution of free needles and syringes and through methadone distribution has not prevented the spread of heroin addiction, curtailed drug-related crime, nor has it proven to decrease the level of HIV infection."

The Dutch harm reduction policy has, however, contributed to more abuse. Dr. Frans Koopsman, public relations director for the Dutch government-funded treatment center "De Hoop," said, "There's no taboo anymore on drug use. For a great part drug use is normalized in the sense that youngsters appear to make no big fuss about using drugs." He reports that adolescent cannabis abuse has doubled since 1990 with perhaps nine percent using pot on a regular basis. He also reports that 80 percent of Dutch criminal activity is linked to drug abuse.

Paul Oldenburger, a Delfzijl businessman, declares, "The war on drugs—we lost it a long time ago." He offered, "These coffee shops, they don't just sell the soft drugs. Hard drugs are available too, and it's an easy step from one to the other.". . .

AMERICA'S HARM REDUCTION DISCIPLES

America's cadre of harm reduction disciples is growing in influence. They have moved into elitist ranks, and many are financed by pro-drug billionaire financier George Soros.

Soros, a Hungarian immigrant worth perhaps $1 billion, reportedly gave away more than $350-million in 1995, the bulk to Eastern European projects. He has invested in American social problems, such as schools, abortion rights, electoral politics, drugs and death. In 1995, he gave $5 million to the American "Project on Death in America" and over the last few years, he has given an estimated $15 million to drug legalization organizations. . . .

Soros declares the drug war lost. In his book, *Soros on Soros*, he says, "I think that the whole idea of eradicating the drug problem is a false idea. . . . A drug-free America is simply not possible. . . . Once you accept this point, you may be able to develop a more rational approach to the problem."

Ethan Nadelmann runs Soros's The Lindesmith Center in New York and is Soros's mouthpiece on drug legalization. Nadelmann told the pro-drug magazine *High Times*, "If by legalization you mean it's time to make marijuana available in a regulated way, then I am for legalization. If you mean that we should pre-scribe heroin for addicts, then, yeah, I am for legalization. If it means that we should legalize the personal use of drugs by adult Americans, well, yeah, I'm for that kind of legalization.". . .

Mr. Soros has also given $6 million to the Washington, D.C.–based Drug Policy Foundation (DPF). Soros supports the DPF, saying, "I do think we need a more open debate [on drugs] and more humane policies in this country. . . . I think the DPF will play a key role in bringing about these changes."

In 1995, the DPF used the money Soros provided to make grants to groups like the Cannabis Action Network in Berkeley, California ($25,000), New York Harm-Reduction Educators ($25,000), the National Organization for the Reform of Mari-juana Laws (NORML) (two grants totaling $23,000), and the Los Angeles–based Clean Needles Now ($25,000).

The DPF frequently hosts Capitol Hill seminars to brief staffers about drug policy. Arnold Trebach, DPF's president and an Ameri-can University professor, showed his harm reduction colors at a Capitol Hill seminar, explaining, "[The] dominant morality is that drug abuse is a greater threat than AIDS." Trebach said the federal government needle-exchange policy is "obscene" be-cause Congress has made the use of taxpayer money for needle giveaways conditional on proof that syringe exchanges reduce the spread of AIDS without encouraging drug abuse.

Clearly, wealthy men like Soros have considerable sway with some politicians. Soros spokesman Nadelmann told *Reason* maga-zine, "The replacement of the Bush administration with the Clinton administration was generally a good thing. It brought in a lot of new blood, new thinking." Even Clinton deputy Secre-tary of State Strobe Talbott has described Soros as "a national re-source—indeed, a national treasure." Whether the mutual admi-ration extends to drug policy remains to be seen. . . .

A FAILED PHILOSOPHY

Harm reduction is a failed philosophy, much as the "safe sex" approach has failed to slow the spread of sexually transmitted diseases among young Americans. A balanced effort to reduce both the supply of and demand for drugs worked in the past and will work again.

II

One hundred years ago, German chemists introduced heroin to the world. On Saturday the New York Academy of Medicine held a conference celebrating the drug's latest use, "heroin maintenance": medically supervised distribution of pure heroin to addicts. The academy's First International Conference on Heroin Maintenance introduces to our shores the latest example of the pernicious drug-treatment philosophy known as "harm reduction."

Harm reduction holds that drug abuse is inevitable, so society should try to minimize the damage done to addicts by drugs (disease, overdose) and to society by addicts (crime, health care costs). According to the Oakland, Calif.-based Harm Reduction Coalition, harm reduction "meets users where they are at . . . accepting for better or worse, that drug use is part of our world."

Its advocates present harm reduction as a rational compromise between the alleged futility of the drug war and the extremism of outright legalization. But since harm reduction makes no demands on addicts, it consigns them to their addiction, aiming only to allow them to destroy themselves in relative "safety"—and at taxpayer expense.

SPECIOUS CHOICE

The recent debate over needle exchange illuminates the political strategy of harm reductionists. First, present the public with a specious choice: Should a drug addict shoot up with a clean needle or a dirty one? (Unquestioned is the assumption that he should shoot up at all.) Then misrepresent the science as Health and Human Services Secretary Donna Shalala did when she pronounced "airtight" the evidence that needle exchange reduces the rate of HIV transmission. In fact, most needle exchange studies have been full of design errors; the more rigorous ones have actually shown an *increase* in HIV infection.

And so it is with heroin maintenance. First, the false dichotomies: pure vs. contaminated heroin, addicts who commit crime to support their habit vs. addicts who don't. Then the distortion of evidence. The Lindesmith Center, one of the conference sponsors, claims that "a landmark Swiss study has successfully maintained heroin addicts on injectable heroin for almost two years, with dramatic reductions in illicit drug use and criminal activity as well as greatly improved health and social adjustment."

In fact, the Swiss "experiment," conducted by the Federal Office of Public Health from 1994 to 1996, was not very scientific. Addicts in the 18-month study were expected to inject themselves with heroin under sterile conditions at the clinic three times a day. They also received extensive counseling, psychiatric services and social assistance (welfare, subsidized jobs, public housing and medical care). Results: The proportion of individuals claiming they supported themselves with illegal income dropped to 10% from 70%; homelessness fell to 1% from 12%. Permanent employment rose to 32% from 14%, but welfare dependency also rose to 27% from 18%. The rate of reported cocaine use among the heroin addicts dropped to 52% from 82%.

These numbers may look promising, but it's hard to know what they mean. Verification of self-reported improvement was spotty at best. And addicts received so many social services—five times more money was spent on them than is the norm in standard treatment—that heroin maintenance itself may have played no role in any overall improvement.

Reprinted by permission of Chuck Asay and Creators Syndicate.

Definitions of success were loose as well. Anyone who kept attending the program, even intermittently, was considered "retained." By this standard, more than two-thirds made it through—a much higher retention rate than in conventional treatment. But considering that the program gave addicts pharmaceutical-grade heroin at little or no cost, it's astonishing that the numbers weren't higher. It turned out that the patients who dropped out were those with the most serious addiction-related problems—those who had been addicted the longest, were the heaviest cocaine users, or had HIV—the very groups that are of the greatest public-health concern.

What's more, the researchers did not compare heroin mainte-nance with conventional treatments such as methadone or resi-dential, abstinence-oriented care. They abandoned their original plan to assign patients randomly to heroin maintenance or con-ventional methadone—because, among other reasons, the sub-jects, not surprisingly, strongly preferred heroin.

"The risk of heroin maintenance is the incentive it provides to 'fail' in other forms of treatment in order to become a publicly supported addict," says Mark Kleiman of UCLA School of Public Policy. And in fact, once the heroin maintenance project started, conventional treatment facilities reported a sharp decline in ap-plications, even though the rate of drug use remained steady.

The Swiss heroin experiment was born out of desperation. In the mid-1980s, the Swiss government became disenchanted with drug treatment and turned to a policy of sanctioned drug use in designated open areas. But this was unsuccessful; the most visible failures being the squalid deterioration of Zurich's Platzspitz Park (the notorious "Needle Park") and the syringe-littered Letten railway station.

It is telling that harm reduction efforts have evolved in coun-tries that provide addicts with a wide array of government bene-fits. Rather than throw up their hands at the poor record of drug rehabilitation, the Swiss and others should acknowledge the ex-tent to which welfare services enable addiction by shielding ad-dicts from the consequences of their actions, financing their drug purchases and encouraging dependency on public largesse.

Nonetheless, Switzerland has ardently embraced heroin maintenance. The Federal Office of Public Health plans to triple enrollment next year to about 3,000; and in 2004 the Swiss Par-liament plans to decriminalize consumption, possession and sale of narcotics for personal use.

Not everyone shares Bern's enthusiasm. Wayne Hall of Aus-tralia's University of New South Wales was an independent eval-uator for the World Health Organization who assessed the ex-perimental plan of the Swiss project. "The unique political context . . . of the trials . . . meant that opportunities were lost for a more rigorous evaluation," he wrote. In February, the In-ternational Narcotics Control Board of the United Nations—a quasijudicial body that monitors international drug treaties—expressed concern that "before [completion of] the evaluation by the World Health Organization of the Swiss heroin experi-ment, pressure groups and some politicians are already promot-ing the expansion of such programmes in Switzerland and their proliferation in other countries."

And indeed, the trials' principal investigator and project directors have traveled to Australia, Austria, Germany, the Netherlands and elsewhere promoting heroin maintenance. They won a sympathetic hearing in the Netherlands, which plans to begin a heroin experiment next month. This isn't surprising; after all, this is a country that has a union for addicts, the Federation of Dutch Junkie Leagues, which lobbies the government for services. In Rotterdam last month, I visited a Dutch Reformed church where the pastor had invited two dealers in to sell discounted heroin and cocaine. He also provided basement rooms where users could inject or smoke heroin.

NOTHING IN RETURN

Even if heroin maintenance "worked"—if it could be proved that heroin giveaways enhanced the addicts' health and productivity—we would still have to confront the raw truth about harm reduction. It is the public-policy manifestation of the addict's dearest wish: to use free drugs without consequence. Imagine extending this model—the use of state-subsidized drugs, the offer of endless social services and the expectation of nothing in return—to America's hard-core addicts.

Today the U.N. General Assembly opens a special session on global drug-control policy. Harm reduction advocates will tell the world body that drug abuse is a human right and that the only compassionate response is to make it safer to be an addict. The Swiss and the Dutch seem to view addicts as irascible children who should be indulged, or as terminally ill patients to be palliated, hidden away and written off. But heroin maintenance is wrong. As an experiment, thus far it is scientifically groundless. As public-health policy it will always be a posture of surrender.

PERIODICAL BIBLIOGRAPHY

The following articles have been selected to supplement the diverse views presented in this chapter. Addresses are provided for periodicals not indexed in the *Readers' Guide to Periodical Literature*, the *Alternative Press Index*, the *Social Sciences Index*, or the *Index to Legal Periodicals and Books*.

Robert Apsler	"Is Drug Abuse Treatment Effective?" *American Enterprise*, March/April 1994.
William J. Bennett and John P. Walters	"Drugs: Face the Facts, Focus on Education," *Insight*, March 6, 1995. Available from 3600 New York Ave. NE, Washington, DC 20002.
David Boyum	"Swift and Sure Sanctions Work Better," *Insight*, June 12, 1995.
Jonathan P. Caulkins	"Treatment Is More Cost-Effective than Law Enforcement," *Insight*, June 12, 1995.
John Cloud	"A Way Out for Junkies?" *Time*, January 19, 1998.
Shelley Donald Coolidge	"In Workplace, Efforts to Nip Drug Abuse Pay Dividends," *Christian Science Monitor*, October 30, 1996.
Mathea Falco	"Drug Prevention Makes a Difference," *USIA Electronic Journal*, June 1997. Available from http://www.usia.gov.
Issues and Controversies On File	"Drug Testing," January 9, 1998. Available from Facts On File News Services, 11 Penn Plaza, New York, NY 10001-2006.
Barry R. McCaffrey	"Drugs and the Media: Communicating in Today's Multi-Media Market," *Vital Speeches of the Day*, August 1, 1998.
Ethan Nadelmann and Jennifer McNeely	"Doing Methadone Right," *Public Interest*, Spring 1996.
William O'Brien, interview by George M. Anderson	"The Crisis in Drug Treatment: An Interview with William O'Brien," *America*, March 16, 1996.
Sally Satel	"Do Drug Courts Really Work?" *City Journal*, Summer 1998. Available from The Manhattan Institute, 52 Vanderbilt Ave., 2nd Fl., New York, NY 10017.
Sally Satel	"For Addicts, Force Is the Best Medicine," *Wall Street Journal*, January 6, 1998.
Christopher S. Wren	"One of Medicine's Best-Kept Secrets: Methadone Works," *New York Times*, June 3, 1997.

SHOULD ILLEGAL DRUGS BE LEGALIZED?

CHAPTER PREFACE

"The first duty of government is to protect its citizens," states the *National Drug Control Strategy*, which also emphasizes that protecting citizens is the goal of U.S. drug policy. However, the report acknowledges that "government must minimize interference in the private lives of citizens," because protecting citizens also means safeguarding their individual freedom. Sometimes these two goals are in conflict: By outlawing certain behaviors—the use of illegal drugs—drug prohibition necessarily curtails individual freedom.

Advocates of drug legalization believe that restricting the use of certain drugs is an unnecessary, unethical, and unconstitutional infringement on individual liberty. They maintain that the government has no right to prohibit substances just because it believes they are unhealthy or immoral. Adam J. Smith, associate director of the Drug Reform Coordination Network, explains this view: "It is beyond the legitimate power of government to use force to control what a free citizen may ingest. . . . There is no more sacred right than the right to control one's body and mind." In matters of personal health, Smith says, "the government may suggest, it may cajole, it may inform, but it must not demand that individuals maintain themselves in accordance with its wishes." Legalization advocates insist that marijuana, cocaine, and heroin should be sold legally, subject to the same types of restriction that regulate the sale and use of alcohol.

However, Theodore Dalrymple, a contributing editor to City *Journal*, rejects the notion of an individual's right to use drugs, arguing that drug use itself reduces a person's freedom: "The idea that freedom is merely the ability to act upon one's whims is surely very thin . . .; a man whose appetite is his law strikes us not as liberated but enslaved." Moreover, drug prohibitionists argue that drug abuse contributes to high rates of child abuse, traffic accidents, and violence. Such behaviors, they say, threaten everyone's right to live in a safe community. The rights of the community must take precedence over personal gratification, says Dalrymple. In his view, "No culture that makes publicly sanctioned self-indulgence its highest good can long survive."

The contributors to the following chapter debate both the moral and practical issues concerning the legalization of drugs and explain what effects they believe legalization would have on crime, public health, and public opinion toward drug use.

|"Individuals have the right to decide for themselves what to put in their bodies."

DRUGS SHOULD BE LEGALIZED

Libertarian Party

The Libertarian Party is a national political party whose members believe in personal responsibility, individual rights, and minimal government. In the following viewpoint, the party argues that drug prohibition causes most drug-related crime. After legalization, the party says, drugs would be more available and thus cheaper. If drugs were cheaper, say the authors, they would be less profitable and drug dealers would no longer resort to violence to defend their trade. Moreover, the party argues that people's civil liberties are violated when the government attempts to crack down on drug users. The authors maintain that although drug abuse is dangerous, individuals have the right to use drugs if they choose.

As you read, consider the following questions:

1. Who profited most from alcohol prohibition in the 1920s, according to the organization?
2. How much of a problem was drug addiction in 1914, in the Libertarian Party's view?
3. How does the Libertarian Party claim America's drug laws originated?

Reprinted from the Libertarian Party, "Should We Relegalize Drugs? Yes," *Pro and Con Direct!* www.nonline.com/procon/html/drugspro.html, May 20, 1997, by permission.

Libertarians, like most Americans, demand to be safe at home and on the streets. Libertarians would like all Americans to be healthy and free of drug dependence. But drug laws don't help, they make things worse.

The professional politicians scramble to make names for themselves as tough anti-drug warriors, while the experts agree that the "war on drugs" has been lost, and could never be won. The tragic victims of that war are your personal liberty and its companion, responsibility. It's time to consider the re-legalization of drugs.

THE LESSONS OF PROHIBITION

In the 1920's, alcohol was made illegal by Prohibition. The result: Organized Crime. Criminals jumped at the chance to supply the demand for liquor. The streets became battlegrounds. The criminals bought off law enforcement and judges. Adulterated booze blinded and killed people. Civil rights were trampled in the hopeless attempt to keep people from drinking.

When the American people saw what Prohibition was doing to them, they supported its repeal. When they succeeded, most states legalized liquor and the criminal gangs were out of the liquor business.

Today's war on drugs is a re-run of Prohibition. Approximately 40 million Americans are occasional, peaceful users of some illegal drug who are no threat to anyone. They are not going to stop. The laws don't, and can't, stop drug use.

Whenever there is a great demand for a product and government makes it illegal, a black market always appears to supply the demand. The price of the product rises dramatically and the opportunity for huge profits is obvious. The criminal gangs love the situation, making millions. They kill other drug dealers, along with innocent people caught in the crossfire, to protect their territory. They corrupt police and courts. Pushers sell adulterated dope and experimental drugs, causing injury and death. And because drugs are illegal, their victims have no recourse.

CRIME AND CIVIL LIBERTIES

Half the cost of law enforcement and prisons is squandered on drug-related crime. Of all drug users, a relative few are addicts who commit crimes daily to supply artificially expensive habits. They are the robbers, car thieves and burglars who make our homes and streets unsafe.

Civil liberties suffer. We are all "suspects", subject to random urine tests, highway check points and spying into our personal finances. Your property can be seized without trial, if the police merely claim you got it with drug profits. Doing business with cash makes you a suspect. America is becoming a police state because of the war on drugs.

Today's illegal drugs were legal before 1914. Cocaine was even found in the original Coca-Cola recipe. Americans had few problems with cocaine, opium, heroin or marijuana. Drugs were inexpensive; crime was low. Most users handled their drug of choice and lived normal, productive lives. Addicts out of control were a tiny minority.

DRUG-RELATED ARRESTS, 1988–95

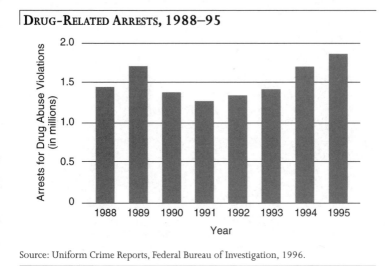

Source: Uniform Crime Reports, Federal Bureau of Investigation, 1996.

The first laws prohibiting drugs were racist in origin—to prevent Chinese laborers from using opium and to prevent blacks and Hispanics from using cocaine and marijuana. That was unjust and unfair, just as it is unjust and unfair to make criminals of peaceful drug users today.

Some Americans will always use alcohol, tobacco, marijuana or other drugs. Most are not addicts, they are social drinkers or occasional users. Legal drugs would be inexpensive, so even addicts could support their habits with honest work, rather than by crime. Organized crime would be deprived of its profits. The police could return to protecting us from real criminals; and there would be room enough in existing prisons for them.

TRY PERSONAL RESPONSIBILITY

It's time to re-legalize drugs and let people take responsibility for themselves. Drug abuse is a tragedy and a sickness. Criminal laws only drive the problem underground and put money in the pockets of the criminal class. With drugs legal, compassionate people could do more to educate and rehabilitate drug users who seek help. Drugs should be legal. Individuals have the right to decide for themselves what to put in their bodies, so long as they take responsibility for their actions.

From the Mayor of Baltimore, Kurt Schmoke, to conservative writer and TV personality, William F. Buckley, Jr., leading Americans are now calling for repeal of America's repressive and ineffective drug laws. The Libertarian Party urges you to join in this effort to make our streets safer and our liberties more secure.

> "We must never back down from the moral message [of drug prohibition]."

DRUGS SHOULD NOT BE LEGALIZED

Dan Quayle

In early 1996, the editors of the conservative magazine *National Review* caused considerable controversy when they announced their support for drug legalization. In the following viewpoint, former vice president Dan Quayle responds to the *National Review*. He says that the problems associated with drug legalization, such as increased drug addiction, would more than outweigh the supposed benefits outlined by the magazine's editors. Moreover, says Quayle, legalizing drugs would remove the moral message against drug use, which is the most effective tool for preventing drug abuse.

As you read, consider the following questions:
1. What is William F. Buckley Jr.'s rationale for legalizing drugs, as paraphrased by the author?
2. According to Quayle, why is the use of alcohol and tobacco by minors pertinent to the argument against drug legalization?
3. Why does Quayle believe that Nancy Reagan's "Just Say No" campaign was effective?

Reprinted from Dan Quayle, "Legalization Argument Is Nothing New," *Conservative Chronicle*, February 14, 1996, by permission of Dan Quayle and Creators Syndicate.

Though rarely praised by elites, *National Review* has been one of the most influential opinion magazines in America since its founding in 1955. The conservative journal is both scholarly and witty, and it often makes predictions with pinpoint accuracy.

That makes it all the more surprising and disappointing that the magazine declares on the cover of its Feb. 12, 1996, issue that "The War on Drugs Is Lost" and that it now favors legalizing drugs.

ATTRACTIVE ARGUMENTS

The editors and contributors argue that the drug war has grown too expensive and is a threat to civil liberties. It is time, they contend, to move toward legalization (at least for adult use) and to focus more resources on treating the problem of addiction.

National Review Editor at Large William F. Buckley Jr. points out that "the pharmaceutical cost of cocaine and heroin is approximately 2 percent of the street price of those drugs." Thus, he concludes, a sharp drop in drug prices under legalization is likely to yield a dramatic reduction in the number of thefts and murders committed by addicts desperate to support their expensive habits. Buckley also foresees an end to the bloody turf battles now fought on city streets by drug merchants.

The legalization argument is nothing new. I've heard it, in some form or another, from the time I first entered public life: "If only we could take the profit out of the drug business, regulate drug quality and be generous in our treatment of addicts, we would finally get ahead of the problem."

Some may find this reasoning attractive, but a look beneath the surface quickly shows that legalization would cause more problems than it would solve.

A MASSIVE INCREASE IN DRUG USE AND ADDICTION

The first result of legalizing drugs would be a massive increase in the number of users throughout the population. This is a simple function of supply and demand: If drugs are simultaneously made cheaper and easier to obtain, more people will try them. And that means more children will do drugs, regardless of whether the law continues to forbid use by minors. As Professor James Q. Wilson of the University of California at Los Angeles wrote in the February 1990 *Commentary*, America's experience with tobacco and alcohol proves that "young people have a way of penetrating markets theoretically reserved for adults."

Increased usage would lead to a second unavoidable consequence of drug legalization: more drug addicts. And, even assuming that lower prices would cause addicts to steal fewer valuables, it is foolish to expect that society would not continue to pay a heavy price for drug-related crimes. Any police officer will tell you that a person on drugs is more likely to neglect a child, abuse a spouse or take a life.

DRUG LEGALIZATION WOULD HARM CHILDREN MOST

Myth: Whether to use drugs and become hooked is an adult decision.

Reality: It is children who choose. Hardly anyone in America begins drug use after age 21. Based on everything known, an individual who does not smoke, use drugs, or abuse alcohol by 21 is virtually certain never to do so. The nicotine pushers understand this, which is why they fight so strenuously to kill efforts to keep their stuff away from kids.

Myth: Legalized drugs would be only for adults and not available to children.

Reality: Nothing in the American experience gives any credence to the ability to keep legal drugs out of the hands of children. It is illegal for them to purchase cigarettes, beer, and liquor. Nevertheless, 3,000,000 adolescents smoke, an average of half a pack a day, constituting a $1,000,000,000-a-year market; and 12,000,000 underage Americans drink, a $10,000,000,000-a-year market.

Joseph A. Califano Jr., *USA Today*, March 1997.

Add to this the societal cost of more traffic accidents, more workplace mishaps and more drug-related emergency-room cases (now at their highest levels ever). And, of course, more crack babies. *National Review's* editors are quick to declare that they do not favor increased drug use; indeed, they explicitly endorse "intensive education of non-users and intensive education designed to warn those who experiment with drugs."

THE MORAL MESSAGE AGAINST DRUG USE

Unfortunately, they ignore a third problem with legalization: How do you scale back drug use—especially among children—when you've removed the moral case against it? In Wilson's eloquent words, "If we believe . . . that dependency on certain mind-altering drugs is a moral issue and that their illegality rests in part on their immorality, then legalizing them undercuts, if it does not eliminate altogether, the moral message."

We must never back down from the moral message. It is the key to ending a scourge that has turned countless lives into nightmares. Nancy Reagan's "Just Say No" campaign was a success for the very reason that it sent a message of uncompromising moral seriousness. No ifs, ands or buts, no Clinton-era jokes about "not inhaling," no musings from a Joycelyn Elders about "studying" legalization.

The Clinton administration has given the drug war low-priority status. Not surprisingly, drug use is on the rise, and studies show that American students have grown less hostile toward illegal drugs.

Clinton's recent choice of four-star Army Gen. Barry McCaffrey to the position of drug czar may signal an election-year conversion to a serious anti-drug strategy. [McCaffrey was sworn in in March 1996.]

If so, I couldn't be more supportive. I only wish the editors of *National Review* were on board as well. They should be applying their considerable talents to developing better ways to fight the drug war rather than waving the white flag of surrender.

| "The illegal drug trade is the country's leading cause of death by homicide—and the illegal drug trade wouldn't exist without prohibition."

LEGALIZING DRUGS WOULD REDUCE CRIME WITHOUT DRAMATICALLY INCREASING DRUG ABUSE

Joshua Wolf Shenk

In the following viewpoint, Joshua Wolf Shenk argues that drugs should be legalized in order to eradicate the illegal drug trade and the violent crime associated with it. Violence among rival drug gangs would be eliminated if drugs were available legally, says the author, and nonviolent drug users would not be deemed criminals. He maintains that drugs should be legalized but their availability should be severely restricted, as is the case with tobacco and alcohol. In addition, the government should continue to sponsor antidrug programs, Shenk contends. Shenk is a contributing editor for the *Washington Monthly*.

As you read, consider the following questions:
1. How do the sentences of nonviolent drug users and dealers compare with those of violent felons, according to Shenk?
2. In Shenk's opinion, why are alcohol and tobacco legal?
3. What evidence does the author provide for his claim that drug use would not rise dramatically following prohibition?

Excerpted from Joshua Wolf Shenk, "Why You Can Hate Drugs and Still Want to Legalize Them," *The Washington Monthly*, October 1995. Reprinted with permission from *The Washington Monthly*. Copyright by The Washington Monthly Company, 1611 Connecticut Ave. NW, Washington, DC 20009, (202) 462-0128.

The choice between two intensely unpleasant options is never easy. But, considering [the drug] problem in all its depth and complexity, it becomes clear that drug prohibition does more harm than good. . . . The fact is we have done a very poor job discouraging drug use with the blunt force of law. The hundreds of billions of dollars spent on drug control in the last several decades have yielded only a moderate decline in the casual use of marijuana and cocaine. But there has been no decrease in hard-core addiction. The total amount of cocaine consumed per capita has actually risen. And even casual use is now creeping up.

COMPARING THE COSTS

Government does have a responsibility to limit the individual and social costs of drug use, but such efforts must be balanced against the harm they cause. And ending the drug war needn't mean a surrender to addiction, or an affirmation of reckless drug use. President Clinton's stance on cigarette addiction—that cigarettes can be both legal and tightly regulated, particularly with respect to advertising aimed at children—points to a middle ground. Potentially, we could do a better job of fighting drug abuse, while avoiding the vicious side-effects of an outright ban.

Unfortunately, this country's discussion of "the drug problem" is marked by little clear analysis and much misinformation. Politicians and bureaucrats minimize or entirely ignore the consequences of prohibition. At the other extreme, libertarians call for government to withdraw from regulating intoxicants entirely. The press, meanwhile, does little to illuminate the costs and benefits of the current prohibition or our many other policy options. "We don't cover drug policy, except episodically as a cops and robbers story," says Max Frankel, the recently retired executive editor of The New York Times. He calls his paper's coverage of the subject "one of my failures there as an editor, and a failure of newspapers generally."

It's not that the consequences of prohibition can't be seen in the newspapers. In the Times in December 1994, for example, Isabel Wilkerson wrote a stirring profile of Jovan Rogers, a Chicago crack dealer who entered the trade when he was 14 and ended up crippled by gunshot wounds. But Wilkerson, as reporters usually do, conveyed the impression that the pathology of the black market is unfortunate, but inevitable—not the result of policies that we can change.

In fact, Rogers' story is a vivid display of the lethal drug trade that prohibition creates, the temptation of bright young men, and the cycle of destruction that soon follows.

For his first job, Rogers got $75 a day to watch out for the police. Soon, he was earning thousands a day. And though Rogers said he began dealing to support his family—"If there's nothing to eat at night," he asked, "who's going to go buy something to make sure something is there? I was the only man in the house"—the big bucks also seized him where, like most teenagers, he was most vulnerable. "If you sell drugs, you had anything you wanted," he said. "Any girl, any friend, money, status. If you didn't, you got no girlfriend, no friends, no money. You're a nothing."

This story is all too common. In communities where two-thirds of the youth lack the schooling or skills to get a decent job, drug dealing is both lucrative and glamorous. Rich dealers are role models and images of entrepreneurial success—the Bill Gateses of the inner city. Unlike straight jobs, though, dealing drugs means entering a world of gruesome violence. Like all initiates, Rogers was issued a gun, and learned quickly to shoot—to discipline other dealers in the gang or to battle rival gangs for control over a corner or neighborhood. Sometimes he would shoot blindly, out of raw fear. Newspapers report stories of "drug-related" murder. But drug *war* murder is more like it. The illegal drug trade is the country's leading cause of death by homicide—and the illegal drug trade wouldn't exist without prohibition. . . .

The high prices caused by prohibition drive crime in another way: Addicts need cash to feed their habits. The junkies I met in New York told me they would spend between $200 and $600 a week for drugs. Melissa, for example, once had a good job and made enough to pay her bills and to buy dope. Then she got laid off and turned to prostitution to support her habit. Others steal to pay for their drugs—from liquor stores, from their families, from dealers, or from other addicts. According to a study by the Bureau of Justice Statistics, one out of every three thefts are committed by people seeking drug money.

This crime wave does not restrict itself to the inner cities. Addicts seeking money to get a fix are very fond of the fine appliances and cash-filled wallets found in wealthier neighborhoods. Suburban high schools may not have swarms of dealers crawling through the fences, but dealers are there too. In fact, the suburbs are increasingly popular for dealers looking to take up residence.

Quite apart from the costs of the black market—the crime, the neighborhoods and lives ruined—Americans also pay a heavy price for the drug war itself. For fiscal 1996, Clinton has requested $14.6 billion for drug control (up from only $1.3 billion in 1983). State and local governments spend about twice that each year.

A NATION BEHIND BARS

But these budgets reflect only a small portion of the costs. In 1980, the United States had 330,000 people in jail; today, it's well over a million, and drug offenders account for 46 percent of that increase. On top of the cost of building prisons, it takes more than $30,000 per year to keep someone in jail. Naturally, prison spending has exploded. The country now spends nearly $30 billion annually on corrections. Between 1970 and 1990, state and local governments hiked prison spending by 232 percent.

Even worse, thanks to mandatory minimum sentences, the system is overloaded with non-violent drug users and dealers, who now often receive harsher penalties than murderers, rapists, and serious white collar criminals. Solicited by an undercover Drug Enforcement Agency (DEA) agent to find a cocaine supplier, Gary Fannon facilitated the deal and received a sentence of life without parole. Larry Singleton raped a teenager, hacked off her arms between the wrist and elbow, and left her for dead in the desert. He received the 14-year maximum sentence and served only eight years. This disparity is not the exception in modern law enforcement. It is the rule. Non-violent drug offenders receive an average 60 months in jail time, *five times* the average 12-month-sentence for manslaughter convicts.

Some people may say: Build more jails. In an era of tax cuts and fiscal freezes, though, every dollar spent on corrections comes from roads, or health care, or education. Even with the huge growth in prison spending, three-fourths of all state prisons were operating over their maximum capacity in 1992. Even conservatives like Michael Quinlan, director of the federal Bureau of Prisons under Ronald Reagan and George Bush, have had enough of this insanity. "They're locking up a lot of people who are not serious or violent offenders," he says. "That . . . brings serious consequences in terms of our ability to incarcerate truly violent criminals."

If sticking a drug dealer in jail meant fewer dealers on the street, perhaps this wave of incarceration would eventually do some good. But it doesn't work like that: Lock up a murderer, and you have one less murderer on the street. Lock up a dealer, and you create a job opening. It's like jailing an IBM executive; the pay is good, the job is appealing, so someone will move into the office before long. Clearing dealers from one neighborhood only means they'll move to another. Busting a drug ring only makes room for a competitor. "We put millions of drug offenders through the courts—and we have more people in jail per capita than any country except Russia—but we're not affecting the drug trade, let alone drug use," says Robert Sweet, U.S. district judge in the Southern district of New York. . . .

Despite these drug war casualties—and the dismal progress in stemming drug use—each year the war intensifies. Politicians

U.S. MURDER RATE
HOMICIDES PER 100,000

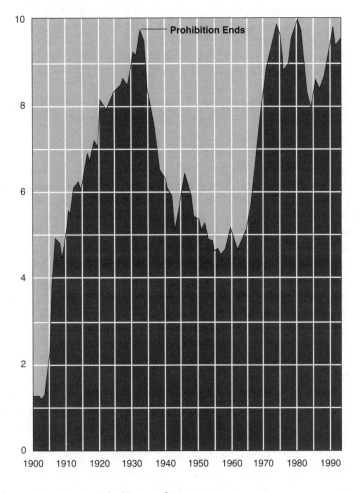

Source: Census Bureau, Federal Bureau of Investigation.

from Newt Gingrich to Bill Bradley now push for expanding the death penalty for dealers. But experience shows that the deterrent effect will be negligible. "There is no evidence that increasing penalties for drug dealing deters people from doing it," says Quinlan. "It just doesn't work like that—not when your chances of getting caught are so low, and the profits are so high." As Quinlan points out, the DEA and White House count it as a success if drug prices are driven up, but that only makes the problem worse. On the streets, meanwhile, we have the worst of both worlds: Drugs are expensive enough to fuel a deadly black market, but people still buy them.

Illegal drugs, left unregulated, are also much more dangerous than they need to be. Imagine drinking whisky with no idea of its potency. It could be 30 proof or 190 proof—or diluted with a dangerous chemical. One addict I met, Mary, had blood-red sores running up her arms—from cocaine cut with meat tenderizer. Virtually all "overdose" deaths from the use of illegal drugs are due to contaminants or the user's ignorance of the drug's potency. "Just desserts," one might say. But isn't the basis of our drug policy supposed to be concern for people's health and well-being? . . .

Cocaine can cause heart attacks in people prone to irregular heartbeats, such as basketball star Len Bias, and seizures in people with mild epilepsy; it's even more dangerous mixed with alcohol and other drugs. Heroin can lead to intense physical dependence—withdrawal symptoms include nausea, convulsions, and loss of bowel control. Even marijuana can be psychologically addictive; smoking too much dope can lead to respiratory problems or even cancer.

Illegal drugs have social costs as well. Consistent intoxication—whether it's a gram-a-day coke fiend, or a regular pot smoker with a miserable memory—can mean lost productivity, increased accidents, and fractured relationships.

And addiction . . . well, it's not pretty. Coke addicts often suffer acute depression without a fix. Heroin is even worse. David Morrison, recalling his furious struggle with heroin addiction in *Washington City Paper*, describes the misery of waiting for his dealer: "If sweet oblivion is the initial carrot, savage withdrawal is the enduring stick. In time, the dope fiend is not so much chasing a high as fleeing a debacle."

Given the terrible consequences of drug abuse, any reasonable person is bound to object: How could we even consider making drugs generally available? But have you asked why alcohol and tobacco are kept generally available?

Tobacco products—linked to cancer of the lungs, throat, larynx, and ovaries—cause 30 percent of all cancer deaths. Even more tobacco-related deaths come from heart attacks and strokes. Every year 435,000 Americans die premature deaths because of cigarettes. And, of course, nicotine is extremely addictive: The Surgeon General has found that the "capture" rate—the percentage of people who become addicted after trying it—is higher with cigarettes than any other drug, legal or illegal. Most nicotine addicts are hooked before age 18.

Alcohol is even more destructive. Extensive drinking often results in bleeding ulcers, cirrhosis of the liver, stomach and intestinal inflammation, and muscle damage as well as severe damage to the brain and nervous system, manifested by blackouts and psychotic episodes.

As for social costs, alcohol is the most likely of all mind-altering substances to induce criminal behavior, according to the National Institute of Justice. Close to 11 million Americans are alcoholics, and another 7 million are alcohol abusers—meaning they've screwed up at work, been in an accident, or been arrested because of drinking. Drunk driving is the cause of a third of all traffic fatalities. Alcohol-related problems affect one out of every four American homes, and alcoholism is involved in 60 percent of all murders and 38 percent of child abuse cases. These statistics only confirm our everyday experience. Who doesn't know of a family shattered by an alcoholic, or someone who has suffered with an alcoholic boss?

LEGALIZATION WITH LIMITS

The reason that alcohol and tobacco are legal, despite the damage they do, is that prohibition would be even worse. In the case of alcohol, we know from experience. The prohibition from 1919 to 1933 is now synonymous with violence, organized crime, and corruption. Financed by huge profits from bootlegging, gangsters like Al Capone terrorized cities and eluded the best efforts of law enforcement. It soon became too much.

After prohibition's repeal, consumption rates for alcohol did in fact rise. But as anyone who was alive in 1933 could tell you, the increase was hardly an explosion. And it seems likely that the rise was fueled by advertising and the movies. Drunks were likeable (bit-player Jack Norton played the amiable falling-down drunk in scores of movies of that era) or even glamorous (like William Powell in The Thin Man films). It took years for government, the media, and entertainers to realize their responsibility to push temperance—and even now they're not doing all they can.

What we have had a hard time learning is that there are a plethora of options between prohibition and laissez-faire. In 1933, after prohibition, the federal government withdrew entirely from regulating the market in spirits. No limits were placed on marketing or advertising, and the siege from Madison Avenue and Hollywood began immediately. For years, the government seemed unable to counter the excesses of legal drug pushers like Philip Morris and Seagrams. Ads for tobacco, beer and liquor dominated the worlds of art and entertainment.

The tide began to turn in 1964, when the Surgeon General issued the first of a series of reports on the dangers of smoking. In 1971 cigarette ads were banned from TV and radio. The media began to open its eyes as well. Meanwhile, there was an equally important change in attitudes. It was once respectable to drink two or three martinis at a business lunch. Today it is not. Nor do we wink at drunk driving or smoking by pregnant women. Cigarette use, in fact, has declined dramatically since the sixties. . . .

The same approach should be employed with now-illegal drugs. An end to prohibition need not mean official endorsement of crack or heroin, but instead could be an opportunity to redouble efforts to limit their use. Drug use would rise after prohibition—but it wouldn't be the catastrophic explosion that drug warriors predict. They count on both distortions of history (claiming an explosion of alcohol use in 1933) and exaggerations of the dangers of cocaine, heroin, and speed—not to mention marijuana and hallucinogens. Though all intoxicants should be taken seriously, these drugs are neither as powerful, addictive, or attractive as many imagine. Among the population of non-users, 97 percent of Americans say they would be "not very likely" or "not at all likely" to try cocaine if it were legal. And even those who would try it in a legal regime would not find themselves immediately in the grip of an insatiable habit. As with alcohol, heavy dependence on cocaine and heroin is acquired over time.

It is a reasonable concern that the disadvantaged would be most vulnerable in a system where drugs are cheap and legally available. But the poor are also the ones paying the heaviest price for prohibition. Most drug users are not poor minorities, but these groups are most affected by the illegal drug trade. "Each of our inner cities has become a bloody Bosnia," writes David Morrison, the journalist and former addict. "But who with the power to make a difference really gives a damn? Having decamped for the suburbs, the middle classes don't have to see the dreadful damage done."

THE BENEFITS OF ELIMINATING THE BLACK MARKET

Of course, lifting prohibition would not be a panacea for our most troubled communities. But imagine the benefits of cutting out the black market. Profit would be eliminated from the drug trade, which means kids wouldn't be drawn to dealing, addicts wouldn't be pushed to thieving, and the sea of violence and crime would ebb. Innocent kids like Launice Smith wouldn't be caught in the crossfire. Students like Jovan Rogers, who survived the drug trade and returned to school, would be less likely to drop out in the first place. And the intense marketing efforts of drug dealers in schoolyards and hallways would stop. (As it stands, dealers encourage users however they can—the more addicts, the more profits for them.)

Meanwhile, police could focus on real crime—and they'd have the prison space to lock up violent or repeat offenders. Businesses, now scared off by inner-city crime, might be drawn back into these communities, and a cycle of recovery could begin. For drug addicts, the federal government could spend the billions now wasted on law enforcement and interdiction to provide effective treatment.

At the same time, the government could clamp down on the alcohol and cigarette corporate behemoths, and make sure that they never get their hands on now-illegal drugs by controlling distribution through package stores—displaying warnings in the stores and on containers themselves. Advertising and marketing, clearly, would be prohibited and government would also have to fund an intensive campaign of public education to prevent misuse, abuse, and addiction.

Beyond government, we must recognize as a culture the damage done by drugs—even if we accept the rights of individuals to use them. The entertainment industry should take this responsibility very seriously. As it is, the scare tactics used by the government give even greater currency to Hollywood's images of the hip, outlaw drug user.

After so many years of prohibition—and a vociferous government effort to distort the truth—it's not hard to imagine why people would fear an epidemic of new drug addicts after prohibition. But such fears are exaggerated. The increase in use could be kept to a minimum by smart public policy. Meanwhile, we would be undoing the horror of present policy—which fractures communities, leaves kids scared to go to the playground, and pushes young men toward death or jail.

With reforms, we could stop this great damage. The good, almost certainly, would far overshadow the new problems created.

Isn't it a moral imperative that we at least try? If legalization proves to be a failure—though the best evidence indicates it would not—we could return to present policy, or find a third way.

Many may be tempted to split the difference—maintain prohibition, but ease some of the penalties. Or legalize the mildest of the illegal drugs, such as marijuana. Or make drugs available to addicts by prescription. There's nothing to prevent experimenting with different strategies. But remember, the tighter the restrictions, the more fuel to the fire of the black market. Undermining the black market has to be the principle of any reform.

ACCEPTING THE REALITY OF DRUG USE

The other temptation is to justify the costs of prohibition in moral terms—"drugs are evil." But pining for a "drug-free America" doesn't change the reality that we'll never have one. Even Lee Brown concedes that the best he can do—with a budget approaching $15 billion—is reduce drug use by 5 percent annually. Is dissuading a few hundred thousand marijuana users worth the terror of the black market?

Ultimately drug policy does come down to tradeoffs. The simple truth is that humans are tempted by intoxicants. And, in a free society like ours, the rights of life and liberty will always be accompanied by people pursuing stiff drinks, or lines of cocaine, or marijuana cigarettes. Inflating the price of drugs through prohibition and jailing sellers and users of drugs sprang from a noble sentiment—that we could eliminate the scourge of addiction, or limit it significantly. Now we know that the enormous efforts in law enforcement have yielded few benefits in curbing drug abuse—and are a paltry disincentive for many drug users and would-be users. The prohibition experiment has failed. The time has come to recognize the great harm it has done. The United States is now akin to a person with poison ivy, scratching furiously at the rashes, and holding fast in denial when they do not go away: Soon, the blood begins to flow. These wounds show themselves every day, in brutal murders and bleak urban landscapes.

We will always have a "drug problem" of some sort. The question is: What kind of drug problem? Ultimately, choosing between regulation and prohibition turns on a simple question: Is it better to allow some individuals to make a bad choice, or to subject many, many innocent people to drive-by shootings, rampant crime, and dangerous schools? The moral policy is to protect the innocent—and then do our best to help the others as well.

| "Making illegal drugs more freely available and more normative will only multiply the drug disaster we already have in our midst."

LEGALIZING DRUGS WOULD NOT REDUCE CRIME AND WOULD DRAMATICALLY INCREASE DRUG ABUSE

Jill Jonnes

Jill Jonnes argues in the following viewpoint that legalizing drugs will not reduce crime, as many legalization advocates suggest. Drugs, not the drug trade, are responsible for many people's anti-social and violent behavior, she says. Legalizing drugs would cause drug use and addiction to skyrocket, she maintains, and the cost of supporting and treating so many addicts would be extraordinary. Finally, writes Jonnes, heroin and crack are much more addicting than alcohol is; the claim that all drugs can be regulated in the same way is specious. Jill Jonnes is the author of *Hep-Cats, Narcs, and Pipe Dreams*, from which this viewpoint is excerpted.

As you read, consider the following questions:

1. Why do people use heroin, according to author Elliott Currie, as quoted by the author?
2. What properties of heroin and cocaine prohibit people addicted to them from leading normal lives, according to Jonnes?
3. Why are there more alcoholics than drug addicts, in the author's opinion?

Why have I—and virtually every other serious student of the American drug scene, whether historian, sociologist, or physician—concluded that legalization is bad policy? Basically because it is the drugs themselves—not the drug laws—that cause the bulk of social harm. One old friend said to me, "Drugs open up your dark side." Making illegal drugs more freely available and more normative will only multiply the drug disaster we already have in our midst. Many of the societal costs generated by the drug culture are caused by the drugs themselves, not the drug laws. . . .

FEAR OF CRIME

Probably the reason most people toy with positive thoughts about legalization is they're tired of worrying about crime, by addicts or by dealers. It's horrible to walk out and find your car window smashed by addicts looking for something to steal. And it's downright scary to drive somewhere and realize that those thuggish young men with the hard stares are drug dealers flagrantly hawking their wares. Presumably they have guns and may well use them just as you're in the wrong trajectory. Drug dealers and their clientele all foster an aura of sordidness and menace. Many middle-class types may find buying drugs in the slums, or copping, part of the excitement and fun, but naturally they would be highly upset if this world got truly near theirs. (Of course, they help perpetuate it. Do they ever think of how their dollars enrich the murderous gangs?)

DRUG USE EXACERBATES CRIMINAL BEHAVIOR

For many, then, the whole raison d'être of legalization would be to eliminate crime and antisocial behavior. Unfortunately, no one who knows the drug scene well believes this would happen. The antisocial behavior isn't caused by the drug laws, it's caused and/or exacerbated by the drugs. What researchers have learned since they began studying the phenomenon of addiction and the drug culture is that "while drug use tends to intensify and perpetuate criminal behavior, it usually does not initiate criminal careers. In fact, the evidence suggests that among the majority of street drug users who are involved in crime, their criminal careers were well established prior to the onset of either narcotics or cocaine use."

Researcher David Nurco, who has spent decades studying heroin addicts in Baltimore, certainly found that most addicts had engaged in criminality before falling in love with heroin. (Only 6 percent were not engaged in any kind of criminal activity at all.) Once hooked, addicts turned more heavily than before to drug dealing, shoplifting, and burglary to finance their habits. The most worrisome—about 7 percent of those studied—was the person the public most fears, the criminal who seems to enjoy committing violent crimes, is very active, and extremely dangerous. In this small group, each acknowledged committing about 900 crimes a year while hooked. But even *before* getting onto heroin, each had committed an average of 573 crimes per year. And even later, once off heroin, each committed 491 crimes a year. While drugs made them worse, they were active criminals who enjoyed committing crimes.

LOWERING DRUG PRICES WILL NOT REDUCE CRIME

The legalizers will no doubt argue that even these violent criminals would commit many fewer crimes if they did not have to pay high prices for heroin. Well, let's look at England, where every effort has been made to provide heroin addicts with cheap legal drugs and keep addicts away from street dealers. Elliott Currie, in his thoughtful book *Reckoning*, writes,

> As we have seen, British addicts could receive prescriptions for heroin from private doctors and, later, from carefully regulated medical clinics. But did addicts who could get heroin legally stop committing crimes? The evidence suggests that many did not—especially after the 1970s, when large numbers of poorer addicts emerged in Britain's cities. Thus a 1979 study of addicts who had been prescribed legal opiates at two London clinics concluded that "treatment for periods of up to 8.5 years had no effect on their overall crime rates." A more recent London study found that most addicts receiving either prescription heroin or methadone continued to commit crimes or to buy heroin in the illicit market.

The reasons that giving out free or cheap heroin and methadone do not necessarily produce completely law-abiding, much less model, citizens, explains Currie, is that "people use heroin not simply to satisfy uncontrollable physical cravings, but as part of their participation in a broader subculture that typically includes several kinds of crime and the use of several other drugs." In short, the fast life of drugs, crime, and general hedonism celebrates drug-taking as part of all-round antisocial behavior, including crime.

But still, let's say that making heroin and crack legal and therefore cheaper or even free would reduce the amount of crime committed per addict. Say, addicts now commit half the crime they once did, as is often true with those on methadone.

Wouldn't that still be better? Think how great it would be if the United States crime rate were even *half* its present high rate?

INCREASED AVAILABILITY LEADS TO INCREASED USE

The fallacy here is assuming that drug use would not balloon once drugs became more freely available. Drug use would only have to double—something that is not hard to imagine—and we would be back where we were because we would now have twice as many addicts, each committing one half as many crimes. Again, let us look at what happened in England—always held up by the legalizers as some kind of beau ideal of a rational approach to drugs. Professor James Q. Wilson explains,

> Until the mid-1960's, British physicians were allowed to prescribe heroin to certain classes of addicts. (Possessing these drugs without a doctor's prescription remained a criminal offense.) For many years this policy worked well enough because the addict-patients were typically middle-class people who had become dependent on opiate painkillers.... There was no drug culture....
>
> All that changed in the 1960's. A few unscrupulous doctors began passing out heroin in wholesale amounts.... A youthful drug culture emerged with a demand for drugs far different from that of older addicts. As a result, the British government required doctors to refer users to government-run clinics to receive their heroin.
>
> But the shift to clinics did not curtail the growth in heroin use. Throughout the 1960's the number of addicts increased— the late John Kaplan of Stanford estimated fivefold—in part as a result of the diversion of heroin from clinic patients to new users on the streets.... Many patients would use some of their maintenance dose and sell the remaining part.... As the clinics learned of this, they began to shift their treatment away from heroin and toward methadone.

Wilson concludes that by the late 1970s, when the number of American heroin addicts had risen tenfold, from fifty thousand to half a million (where it has remained stable), that "the number of British addicts increased by thirtyfold in ten years: the actual increase may have been much larger.... In the early 1980s the numbers began to rise again, and this time nobody doubted that a real epidemic was at hand. The increase was estimated to be 40 percent a year." The lesson here is that the more available heroin is, the more people will use it. Events in Pakistan show the same pattern. Pakistan had no noticeable problem with heroin, but it developed a huge problem in five years—1.3 million addicts—simply because heroin was widely available.

Drug Addicts Are Not Productive Members of Society

Moreover, those who propose legalization or making drugs more easily available to addicts in order to minimize crime somehow assume that once addicts have all the drugs they need, that will be that. But the pharmacology of the two "hard" drugs—heroin and cocaine—mitigate against any normalcy. Professor James Inciardi has spent decades hanging around addicts and drug scenes. He says, "Because heroin is a short-acting drug, with its effects lasting at best four to six hours, it must be taken regularly and repeatedly. Because there is more rapid onset when taken intravenously, most heroin users inject the drug. Because heroin has depressant effects, a portion of the user's day is spent in a semi-stupified state. Collectively, these attributes result in a user more concerned with drug-taking and drug-seeking than health, family, work, relationships, responsibility, or anything else." Crack cocaine is not a depressant, but a stimulant. Its serious devotees generally use it in a binging pattern. They snort or smoke for hours and even days to maintain the euphoria before collapsing into sleep. High doses of cocaine can bring on violent behavior, psychosis, strokes, and heart attacks. It's hard to imagine someone supplied with however much cocaine or crack they want making much of an employee for anyone.

Redefining Crime Instead of Reducing It

Legalization would decrease drug distribution crime because most of those activities would become lawful. But would legalization necessarily reduce other drug-related crime like robbery, rape, and assault? Presumably legalization would reduce the cost of drugs and thus addicts might commit fewer crimes to pay for their habits. But less expensive drugs might also feed their habit better, and more drugs means more side effects like paranoia, irritability and violence. Suggestions that crime can somehow be eliminated by redefining it are spurious.

Robert L. Maginnis, *Insight*, March 1995.

So we might well supply addicts with large quantities of drugs, but it would certainly make them even less employable than they already are. And they would still need money to pay the rent and buy food, clothes, and other necessities. Where would this money come from if they did not work? At the moment, the U.S. taxpayer *already* provides sufficient money to underwrite illegal drug habits to about 250,000 addicts and alcoholics. How is this? Because Congress decided back in 1972 that if you were too drunk or strung out to work, then you were eligible for Social Security disability payments. Few addicts were aware of this until the 1990s, but once they were, then the numbers tripled. Two thirds of the $1.4 billion disbursed annually to this group in 1994 went straight to the addicts and alcoholics, who were not required to enter treatment to qualify for help. These monthly infusions of taxpayer cash were squandered largely on drugs and drink, say local social workers and treatment counselors, making it very difficult to get addicts into treatment. This federal cash for addicts may well end soon, since being revealed and denounced by Senator William S. Cohen of Maine.

To envision America with even more easily and cheaply available heroin and crack, just imagine even larger armies of homeless. Pete Hamill describes the unpleasant public consequence as experienced in the city with the nation's biggest drug culture, New York: "They are everywhere: rummies and junkies, most of them men, their bodies sour from filth and indifference. They sleep in subways and parks, in doorways and in bank lobbies. Some chatter away with the line of con that's learned in the yards of prisons. . . . Some are menacing and dangerous, their requests for handouts essentially demands." This segment of the so-called homeless want to preserve whatever funds they get from panhandling or stealing for one thing—a fix of drugs and alcohol. Even if drugs cost nothing, these people would still be noxious public burdens. And there would be many, many more of them, still panhandling and committing crimes.

ADDICTS REQUIRE ESCALATING DOSAGES

But presume that despite all this, society still wanted to hand out drugs to addicts. There are yet other practical problems. The reality is that most hard-core drug addicts are polydrug abusers who simply want to get high. And because the body daily develops more tolerance for abused drugs, addicts must use escalating dosages to achieve euphoria. This is pharmacological reality. Will we hand out ever increasing doses of heroin and cocaine and whatever else is requested each week to individual drug abusers? If not, the addicts' ever growing appetites will not be satisfied and they will get supplementary fixes from street dealers.

If we do hand out increasing doses, what will happen when inevitably addicts die of overdoses? We live in a highly litigious society. It doesn't take much imagination to dream up all the possible lawsuits—from ODs to drug-exposed babies. Any policeman or emergency room doctor can attest that cocaine in large doses can incite psychotic, violent behavior. Are we prepared to be responsible for the behavior of those we supply with legal cocaine? The practical problems in providing these extremely destructive drugs are insurmountable.

The Case of Alcohol

And then, of course, there is the eternal refrain: Well, look at alcohol, it causes much more harm than drugs. Yes and no. Alcohol certainly causes many health-related problems and actual deaths. But this is again getting stuck in the public health mindset that only measures problems by "morbidity and mortality." This ignores the huge antisocial problems generated and exacerbated by drugs, because those don't register on public health measurements.

Alcohol is classed as a "moderately reinforcing" drug. Heroin and cocaine are "highly reinforcing." If all these substances were equally available, there would almost certainly be more drug addicts than alcoholics simply because of the more addicting nature of heroin and cocaine. Right now in this country we have about 10 million alcoholics. Why so many? Because this is a *legal* drug, one readily available throughout the nation—whether big city, suburb, or rural town. Although the sale of alcohol certainly comes under certain strictures and rules, you can almost always find a bar or a liquor store. We have five hundred thousand heroin addicts and 2 million cocaine addicts. Why so few compared to the less addictive alcohol? Because these are *illegal* substances. Finding them is not easy and certainly not safe.

A demonstration of how reinforcing cocaine is versus alcohol is seen in a one-year follow-up study done of sixty-five cocaine abusers treated at the Sierra Tucson center in Arizona: "The population consisted primarily of single, male, white cocaine abusers with relatively short drug histories. Overall, 45 percent of the cocaine abusers treated in the program gave self-reports of achieving one year of abstinence successfully, compared to 75 percent of the alcoholics graduating from the program."

Most Americans Rightly Fear Drug Legalization

I find nothing hypocritical about limited and controlled access to alcohol. An important distinction between alcohol and the illegal drugs is that while it is possible to abuse all of them, anyone who is using drugs is seeking strictly to get high. This is not true with alcohol. On any given evening in America, tens of millions come home and unwind with a glass of wine or beer or a martini. Are they seeking to get high? Not if they're having one or two glasses. This commonsense distinction between how alcohol is used widely (to relax, for the pleasure of the taste of the stuff) and how illegal drugs are used (to get high) makes alcohol much more socially acceptable. Prohibition made clear that the majority of Americans wanted it that way. In states where the majority don't, they still have Prohibition. But there has never emerged a majority in this country asking to have the far more dangerous heroin and cocaine made legal. Even the "moderately reinforcing" marijuana never could garner a significant social movement.

It's really a shame that virtually all public debate about the drug problem is dominated by the phony issue of drug legalization or decriminalization. I say that because there is not the remotest political prospect that such a thing will ever come to pass. The reality is that the great mass of Americans rightly fear illegal drugs and want them kept as far away as possible. If that means violent drug markets are confined to (and ruining) inner-city neighborhoods and prisons are filled to bursting, middle-class Americans accept that price. All they know is heroin and cocaine are not available at the local mall. The highly public energy devoted to half-baked legalization proposals should be focused on shrinking the drug culture, especially the big hard-core drug population whose habits have become a major factor in the spread of AIDS.

PERIODICAL BIBLIOGRAPHY

The following articles have been selected to supplement the diverse views presented in this chapter. Addresses are provided for periodicals not indexed in the *Readers' Guide to Periodical Literature*, the *Alternative Press Index*, the *Social Sciences Index*, or the *Index to Legal Periodicals and Books*.

Joseph A. Califano Jr.   "Legalization of Narcotics: Myths and Reality," *USA Today*, March 1997.

Thomas W. Clark   "Keep Marijuana Illegal—for Teens," *Humanist*, May/June 1997.

Theodore Dalrymple   "Don't Legalize Drugs," *City Journal*, Spring 1997. Available from The Manhattan Institute, 52 Vanderbilt Ave., 2nd Fl., New York, NY 10017.

Dirk Chase Eldredge   "Would Legalizing Drugs Serve America's National Interest?: Yes," *Insight*, September 14, 1998. Available from 3600 New York Ave. NE, Washington, DC 20002.

Erich Goode   "Strange Bedfellows: Ideology, Politics, and Drug Legalization," *Society*, May/June 1998.

Issues and Controversies On File   "Drug Legalization," March 8, 1996. Available from Facts On File News Services, 11 Penn Plaza, New York, NY 10001-2006.

National Review   "War on Drugs Is Lost," special section, February 12, 1996.

Paul B. Stares   "Drug Legalization: Time for a Real Debate," *Brookings Review*, Spring 1996.

R. Emmett Tyrrell Jr.   "The Badly Flawed Case for Legalizing Drugs," *Conservative Chronicle*, February 21, 1996. Available from PO Box 29, Hampton, IA 50441.

Theodore Vallance   "A Most Complex Problem," *World & I*, January 1995. Available from 3600 New York Ave. NE, Washington, DC 20002.

Walter Wink   "Getting Off Drugs: The Legalization Option," *Friends Journal*. Available from 1216 Arch St., 2A, Philadelphia, PA 19107-2835.

Mortimer B. Zuckerman   "Great Idea for Ruining Kids," *U.S. News & World Report*, February 24, 1997.

FOR FURTHER DISCUSSION

CHAPTER 1

1. Seth Stevenson contends that the government's media campaign against drug abuse exaggerates the dangers of drugs. Stevenson believes the ads lie by teaching children that, as he puts it, "all drug use leads to disaster." Do you think it is wrong for the government to make this claim? Explain your answer.

2. The National Center on Addiction and Substance Abuse argues that teen drug use is increasing, while Mike Males claims that adult drug abuse is a much more serious problem than teen drug use. Based on the two viewpoints, do you think increased efforts to reduce teen drug use are necessary? Why or why not?

3. Both the Center for Substance Abuse Prevention and the National Organization for the Reform of Marijuana Laws use statistics to support their claims about the gravity of teen marijuana use. Whose evidence is more persuasive, and why?

CHAPTER 2

1. Katherine Kersten maintains that, contrary to its intended goal, the Drug Abuse Resistance Education (DARE) program might actually increase teenage drug use. According to Kersten's son, DARE "makes you want to try drugs, to see what they're like." How might a proponent of drug education respond to this comment?

2. According to Brad Owen, antidrug advertising discourages teenagers from using drugs. Ryan H. Sager, on the other hand, contends that such media campaigns are objects of ridicule among teens. Whose argument is more persuasive? Why?

3. The Office of National Drug Control Policy provides statistics supporting the effectiveness of drug treatment programs. Do you find these statistics convincing, or do you agree with Fred Reed's contention that the effectiveness of drug rehabilitation has not been proven? Explain your answer.

CHAPTER 3

1. Joseph McNamara uses the term "war on drugs" throughout his viewpoint. However, Barry R. McCaffrey believes that the phrase is a poor metaphor for U.S. drug policy. Do you think the metaphor is appropriate? Explain your answer.

2. U.S. drug policy consists of several different strategies: domestic law enforcement, antidrug education and prevention efforts, treatment for addicts, interdiction of drugs entering the

country, and destruction of international drug trafficking organizations and sources of supply. None of the authors in this chapter, however, give equal treatment to all these parts of U.S. drug strategy. Which drug policy programs do Joseph McNamara, Barry R. McCaffrey, David Boaz, and Charles E. Grassley emphasize the most? Why do you think each author may have focused on some aspects of drug policy and avoided others?

3. Harm reduction policies do not condemn drug use but seek only to reduce the harm that drug abuse causes. Current drug strategies, on the other hand, could be termed "use reduction" policies since they aim to reduce all illegal drug use. Which type of policy do you think is best? Do you think that both approaches can be incorporated into U.S. drug policy, or are the philosophies too contradictory? Harm reduction has been called the "safe sex" approach to drug abuse. In what ways is this analogy appropriate or inappropriate?

Chapter 4

1. The Libertarian Party insists that individuals should decide for themselves whether or not to use drugs. Dan Quayle believes that drug prohibition is vital to the moral message that drug abuse is wrong. Which view do you agree with? Does Quayle's assertion that legalizing drugs would increase drug use among minors affect your opinion? How might the Libertarian Party respond to the claim that drug prohibition is necessary for children's sake?

2. One of the main arguments against legalizing drugs is that legalization would lead to a huge increase in drug abuse. How does Joshua Wolf Shenk refute this claim? Is his argument convincing? Compare his comments about the dangers of cocaine and heroin with Jill Jonnes's. Whose are most persuasive?

3. Both Jill Jonnes and Joshua Wolf Shenk use America's experience with alcohol to predict the effects that legalizing other drugs would have. Based on the viewpoints, do you think marijuana, cocaine, or heroin can be controlled in the same way that alcohol and tobacco are? Explain your answer.

ORGANIZATIONS TO CONTACT

The editors have compiled the following list of organizations concerned with the issues debated in this book. The descriptions are derived from materials provided by the organizations. All have publications or information available for interested readers. The list was compiled on the date of publication of the present volume; the information provided here may change. Be aware that many organizations take several weeks or longer to respond to inquiries, so allow as much time as possible.

Canadian Centre on Substance Abuse (CCSA)
75 Albert St., Suite 300, Ottawa, ON K1P 5E7, CANADA
(613) 235-4048 • fax: (613) 235-8101
e-mail: admin@ccsa.ca • website: http://www.ccsa.ca

Established in 1988 by an Act of Parliament, CCSA works to minimize the harm associated with the use of alcohol, tobacco, and other drugs. It disseminates information on the nature, extent, and consequences of substance abuse; sponsors public debates on the topic; and supports organizations involved in substance abuse treatment, prevention, and educational programming. The center publishes the newsletter *Action News* six times a year.

Drug Enforcement Administration (DEA)
700 Army Navy Dr., Arlington, VA 22202
(202) 307-1000
website: http://www.usdoj.gov/dea/

The DEA is the federal agency charged with enforcing the nation's drug laws. The agency concentrates on stopping the smuggling and distribution of narcotics in the United States and abroad. It publishes the *Drug Enforcement Magazine* three times a year.

Drug Policy Foundation
4455 Connecticut Ave. NW, Suite B500, Washington, DC 20008-2328
(202) 537-5005 • fax: (202) 537-3007
e-mail: dpf@dpf.org • website: http://www.dpf.org

The foundation supports the creation of drug policies that respect individual rights, protect community health, and minimize the involvement of the criminal justice system. It supports legalizing many drugs and increasing the number of treatment programs for addicts. Publications include the bimonthly *Drug Policy Letter* and the book *The Great Drug War*. It also distributes *Press Clips*, an annual compilation of newspaper articles on drug legalization issues, as well as legislative updates.

Join Together
441 Stuart St., 7th Fl., Boston, MA 02116
(617) 437-1500 • fax: (617) 437-9394
e-mail: info@jointogether.org • website: http://www.jointogether.org

Founded in 1991, Join Together supports community-based efforts to reduce, prevent, and treat substance abuse. They publish community action kits to facilitate grassroots efforts to increase awareness of substance abuse issues as well as a quarterly newsletter.

Lindesmith Center
400 W. 59th St., New York, NY 10019
(212) 548-0695 • fax: (212) 548-4670
website: http://www.lindesmith.org

The Lindesmith Center is a policy research institute that focuses on broadening the debate on drug policy and related issues. The center houses a library and information center; organizes seminars and conferences; acts as a link between scholars, government, and the media; directs a grant program in Europe; and undertakes projects on topics such as methadone policy reform and alternatives to drug testing in the workplace. The center publishes fact sheets on topics such as needle and syringe availability, drug prohibition and the U.S. prison system, and drug education.

National Center on Addiction and Substance Abuse at Columbia University (CASA)
152 W. 57th St., 12th Fl., New York, NY 10019
(212) 841-5200 • fax: (212) 956-8020
website: http://www.casacolumbia.org

CASA is a private nonprofit organization that works to educate the public about the costs and hazards of substance abuse and the prevention and treatment of all forms of chemical dependency. The center supports treatment as the best way to reduce chemical dependency. It produces publications describing the harmful effects of alcohol and drug addiction and effective ways to address the problem of substance abuse.

National Institute on Drug Abuse (NIDA)
U.S. Department of Health and Human Services
5600 Fishers Ln., Rockville, MD 20857
website: http://www.nida.nih.gov

NIDA supports and conducts research on drug abuse—including the yearly Monitoring the Future Survey—to improve addiction prevention, treatment, and policy efforts. It publishes the bimonthly *NIDA Notes* newsletter, the periodic *NIDA Capsules* fact sheets, and a catalog of research reports and public education materials such as *Marijuana: Facts for Teens*.

BIBLIOGRAPHY OF BOOKS

David Sadofsky Baggins — *Drug Hate and the Corruption of American Justice.* Westport, CT: Praeger, 1998.

Dan Baum — *Smoke and Mirrors: The War on Drugs and the Politics of Failure.* Boston: Little, Brown, 1996.

William Bennett — *Body Count: Moral Poverty—and How to Win America's War Against Crime and Drugs.* New York: Simon & Schuster, 1996.

Eva Bertram et al. — *Drug War Politics: The Price of Denial.* Berkeley and Los Angeles: University of California Press, 1996.

Warren K. Bickel and Richard J. DeGrandpre, eds. — *Drug Policy and Human Nature.* New York: Plenum Press, 1996.

Vincent T. Bugliosi — *The Phoenix Solution: Getting Serious About Winning America's War on Drugs.* Beverly Hills, CA: Dove, 1996.

Lawrence Clayton — *Working Together Against Drug Addiction.* New York: Rosen, 1996.

Scott Dowling, ed. — *The Psychology and Treatment of Addictive Behavior.* Madison, CT: International Universities Press, 1995.

Diana R. Gordon — *The Return of the Dangerous Classes: Drug Prohibition and Policy Politics.* New York: W.W. Norton, 1994.

Mike Gray — *Drug Crazy: How We Got into This Mess and How We Can Get Out.* New York: Random House, 1998.

Mary R. Haack, ed. — *Drug-Dependent Mothers and Their Children: Issues in Public Policy and Public Health.* New York: Springer, 1997.

James I. Inciardi et al. — *Drug Control and the Courts.* Thousand Oaks, CA: Sage, 1996.

Jill Jonnes — *Hep-Cats, Narcs, and Pipe Dreams: A History of America's Romance with Illegal Drugs.* New York: Scribner, 1996.

Cynthia Kuhn et al. — *Buzzed: The Straight Facts About the Most Used and Abused Drugs from Alcohol to Ecstasy.* New York: W.W. Norton, 1998.

Richard S. Lee and Mary Lee — *Drugs and the Media.* New York: Rosen, 1994.

Glenn A. Levant — *Keeping Kids Drug Free: D.A.R.E. Official Parents Guide.* San Diego: Thunder Bay Press, 1998.

Robert L. Maginnis — *Addicts in "Paradise."* Washington, DC: Family Research Council, 1996.

Robert L. Maginnis	*Legalization of Drugs: The Myths and the Facts.* Washington, DC: Family Research Council, 1995.
Kenneth J. Meier	*The Politics of Sin: Drugs, Alcohol, and Public Policy.* Armonk, NY: M.E. Sharpe, 1994.
Richard Lawrence Miller	*Drug Warriors and Their Prey: From Police Power to Police State.* Westport, CT: Praeger, 1996.
National Center on Addiction and Substance Abuse	*Legalization: Panacea or Pandora's Box.* New York: National Center on Addiction and Substance Abuse, 1995.
David E. Newton	*Drug Testing: Protecting Society or Invading Privacy.* Springfield, NJ: Enslow, 1998.
Office of National Drug Control Policy	*National Drug Control Strategy 1998.* Washington, DC: U.S. Government Printing Office, 1998. Available from http://www.whitehousedrugpolicy.gov.
Anne Marie Pagliaro and Louis A. Pagliaro	*Substance Use Among Children and Adolescents: Its Nature, Extent, and Effects from Conception to Adulthood.* New York: John Wiley, 1996.
Craig Reinarman and Harry G. Levin, eds.	*Crack in America: Demon Drugs and Social Justice.* Berkeley and Los Angeles: University of California Press, 1997.
Ed Rosenthal and Steve Kubby	*Why Marijuana Should Be Legal.* New York: Thunder's Mouth Press, 1996.
Elizabeth A. Ryan	*Straight Talk About Drugs and Alcohol.* New York: Facts On File, 1995.
Jeffrey A. Schaler, ed.	*Drugs: Should We Legalize, Decriminalize, or Deregulate?* Amherst, NY: Prometheus, 1998.
Elizabeth Schleichert	*Marijuana.* Springfield, NJ: Enslow, 1996.
Marc A. Schuckit	*Educating Yourself About Alcohol and Drugs: A People's Primer.* New York: Plenum Press, 1998.
Laura Stamper	*When the Drug War Hits Home: Healing the Family Torn Apart by Teenage Drug Abuse.* Minneapolis: Fairview Press, 1997.
Paul B. Stares	*Global Habit: The Drug Problem in a Borderless World.* Washington, DC: Brookings Institution, 1996.
Thomas Szasz	*Our Right to Drugs: The Case for a Free Market.* New York: Syracuse University Press, 1996.
United Nations International Drug Control Programme	*World Drug Report.* New York: Oxford University Press, 1997.
William Weir	*In the Shadow of the Dope Fiend: America's War on Drugs.* New Haven, CT: Archon, 1995.

INDEX

advertising campaigns
  can deter drug abuse by teens, 75–78
    con, 79–82
  and public service announcements
    funding for, 93
AIDS/HIV
  effects of needle exchange programs
    on, 132
  efforts to combat, in Holland,
    118–19, 128
  and IV drug use, 119
alcohol
  deaths related to, 95
  DUI arrest and prosecution costs, 21
  as gateway drug, 28
  is less addictive than heroin or
    cocaine, 163
  problematic use of, 18
  social costs of, 153
American Civil Liberties Union
  (ACLU), 68
American Management Association, 62
American Psychologist, 13
"America's War on Drugs—Searching
  for Solutions" (ABC news magazine),
  127
Apsler, Robert, 89
Armentano, Paul, 45
arrests
  drug-related, 105, 141
  on marijuana charges, 123

Baan Commission, 123
Bertram, Eva, 12
Bias, Len, 152
black market
  benefits of eliminating, 155
  cost of drugs on, 149–50
Boaz, David, 104
Botvin, Gilbert, 60
Brandeis, Louis, 70
Brophy, Chris, 59
Brown, Lee, 156
Brown, Sandra R., 13
Bruneau, Julie, 129
Buckley, William F., Jr., 108, 127, 142,
  144
Bush, George, 96

Califano, Joseph A., Jr., 145
cannabis
  use among teens in U.S. vs.

Netherlands, 120, 123–24
  see also marijuana
Cannabis Action Network, 131
Carter, Jimmy, 48
Center for Substance Abuse Prevention,
  38
Centers for Disease Control (CDC)
  on HIV and IV drug use, 119
China
  introduction of opium to, 95
civil liberties
  drug prohibition violates, 107–108,
    140–41
Clayton, Richard, 58
Clinton, Bill, 80, 99, 102
  administration of, 131
    anti-marijuana campaign of, 123
    shift of drug policy under, 127–28,
      146
  stance on tobacco regulation, 148
cocaine
  addictiveness of, 163
  dangers of, 152
  pharmaceutical cost vs. street price of,
    144
  price stability of, 96
  traffickers created demand for, 114–15
  users of, are not productive, 161
Cohen, William S., 162
Commentary, 144
Condrone, Kerry, 129
Conyers, John, 47
Crier, Catherine, 127
crime
  drug prohibition causes, 105–106
  drug use exacerbates, 158–59
  and substance abuse, 19–21
Cronkite, Walter, 37
Current, William F., 63
Currie, Elliott, 159

Dalrymple, Theodore, 138
deaths
  from drug overdoses, 33, 35
  from drug-related violence, 37
domestic violence
  is linked with substance abuse, 18–19
Donnermeyer, Joseph F., 55
driving under the influence (DUI)
  arrest and prosecution costs for, 21
Drug Abuse Resistance Education
  (DARE)

M8224-TN

87